THE FORM OF MAN

BRILL's STUDIES IN INTELLECTUAL HISTORY

THE FORM OF MAN

HUMAN ESSENCE IN SPINOZA'S *ETHIC*

BY

LUCIA LERMOND

E.J. BRILL

LEIDEN • NEW YORK • KØBENHAVN • KÖLN

1988

LIBRARY OF CONGRESS
Library of Congress Cataloging-in-Publication Data

Lermond, Lucia.
    The form of man: human essence in Spinoza's Ethic/by Lucia
Lermond.
        p.   cm.—(Brill's studies in intellectual history, ISSN
0920-8607; v. 11)
    Bibliography: p.
    Includes index.
    ISBN 90-04-08829-6
    1. Spinoza, Benedictus de, 1632-1677. Ethica. 2. Ethics—Early
works to 1800. I. Title. II. Series.
B3974.L47   1988
170—dc19   88-5039
                                                                    CIP

ISSN 0920-8607
ISBN 90 04 08829 6

PRINTED IN THE NETHERLANDS BY E. J. BRILL

For the teacher with whom I first studied Spinoza,
Harvey Burstein.
κοινὰ γὰρ τὰ τῶν φίλων.
'Since friends have all things in common.'

CONTENTS

PREFACE

Spinoza's *Ethica* gives us an ethic 'ordine geometrico demonstrata.' Here, Spinoza's use of the geometrical method suggests two things: the unity of nature and the power of the mind to grasp this unity. These truths are not tied to the geometrical method, which Spinoza employed also in his exposition of Descartes' philosophy. Yet, the geometrical method lays open a pattern of interrelated ideas, and, demanding, as it does, continual recapitulation, brings us into control of a more and more complex unity. The *Ethic* reflects the unity of nature and the union of the mind with unity.

Conceiving his work as analogue of self-causing substance, Spinoza intended that the *Ethic* be sufficient to itself. We believe that the *Ethic* does, indeed, generate the intelligibility of its own terms. In confining itself to textual analysis, our study makes this claim.

This is thus a study of the *Ethic in se*. We support all interpretive claims by reference to statements contained in that work alone, following Spinoza's practice of parenthetic reference within the body of the text. Brief quotes are similarly identified. Longer citations appear in English with identification and in Latin with location by volume, page, and first line in *Spinoza Opera*, ed. Carl Gebhardt (Heidelberg: C. Winter, 1925). We have utilized the English translation of W. H. White, published in *Spinoza Selections*, ed. John Wild (New York: Charles Scribner's Sons, 1958). Where Spinoza's own supporting references have been omitted from the quotations, this has been indicated by ellipsis.

We have purposely resisted the temptation to develop our interpretation of the *Ethic* using material from other portions of Spinoza's oeuvre. Upon occasion, we refer to these other works, identifying them in the notes. All discussion of the critical literature has been reserved for the end-notes.

Notes referring the reader to other texts and to secondary sources are not intended to be exhaustive. They merely suggest the concerns of the author of this study and point out possible areas of exploration.

INTRODUCTION

We feel and know by experience that we are eternal.   (schol. prop. 23, V)

Sentimus experimurque, nos aeternos esse.   (II, 252, 4)

In his doctrine of the eternity of the human mind, Spinoza defines man. The meaning of man is realized in that ordering and emendation of intellect demonstrated by the *Ethic* itself, for logical proofs are the 'eyes of the mind' by which it sees, and conception, the sensibility of mind (schol. prop. 23, V). Thus, the *Ethic* gives us the 'form of man,' the meaning of human essence as mode grounded in the infinite substance of divine essence, by explicating the ontic force of its own method.

For Spinoza, method concerns the understanding of truth, that is, the self-confirming nature of the true idea. Method may be identified with *idea ideae*, the idea of the idea, insofar as *idea ideae* describes the essence of consciousness: the genetic power of thought, the power of thought as medium of its own generation. At its most primitive, at its most impotent, thought is defined by this potency.

For complex human being, *idea ideae* involves a self-awareness that finds it consummation in certainty. It is the power to feel, to experience, finally, to understand. Ontically grounded, it is authentic interaction with the actual. To think is to interact with the meaning of things. A thing thus 'means' what it is, from its own perspective as exercise of essence, from the perspective of the other as being that may nourish or debilitate. Man is a part of nature, and Spinoza's development of the intrinsic activity of rational thought cannot be divorced from his insistence upon the necessarily genetic or causal nature of adequate definition. A 'concept' is agency. Man's mind is the meaning of man. Enworlded, he struggles to achieve himself as he strives to know the value of things.

Yet, man is a one within a One, and the meaning of man, a moment in the meaning of the world: the idea of God.

In the fifth book of the *Ethic*, Spinoza presents his doctrine of the immortality of the mind through participation in the eternity of divine intelligence. It is in terms of this doctrine that the *Ethic* must ultimately be understood. As Spinoza himself argues, the order of reason that he has set forth can be grasped apart from the doctrine of the mind's eternity (prop. 41, V), but this merely displays the difference between reason and intuitive science and does not vitiate their continuity. Man's rationality finds fruition in the beatitude of divine love, in the glory of God (schol. prop. 36, V).

In the *Ethic*, Spinoza prefers the term 'eternity' to 'immortality,' seeking thereby to affirm the absolutely non-durational character of the eternal. Yet 'immortal' remains accurate appellation. It is not time that unmakes man. Knowledge alone is the limit of the mind. This is Spinoza's teaching: For those that love the Living God, there is no death.

CHAPTER ONE

THE PROBLEM OF HUMAN ESSENCE

Spinoza declares the goal of the *Ethic* knowledge of the human mind and its utmost beatitude (intro., II). In our interrogation of this work, we have been driven again and again to the problem of human essence. What is the 'form of man' (prop. 10, II)? Specifically, we have found ourselves concerned with the import of human essence in Spinoza's theory of individuals and universals. This ontological question has proved intimately related both to his epistemology and to his doctrine of immortality.

In examination of Spinoza's claims about human essence, we have realized that they compose a profound meditation upon the nature of the one and the many. Spinoza's 'form of man' is his account of the one and the many, and its significance for a finite individual.

Our study takes this as its basis and is delimited by our attempt to manifest the one and the many in the meaning of human essence.

From Spinoza's *natura naturans/natura naturata* distinction, we derive the principle of the indivisibility/infinite divisibility of substance. Unity and infinity are necessary correlates in the perfect puissance of the divine nature. Fully realized potency, God's creativity is absolute and constitutive. In this inviolable one of creative being, all beings are interrelated.

The being of being is eternity itself, as the infinite activity of *causa sui*. Eternity engenders all durational individuals. All durational individuals interconnect in the nexus of God's efficacy. Here, the necessity of the divine nature issues in the necessary determination of the modes. The mutable depends for being upon the immutable.

In the conception of *causa sui*, Spinoza presents in germ the ontological argument of the *Ethic*. One knows the being of *causa sui* by virtue, by force, of its existence. Its 'nature cannot be conceived unless existing,' 'non potest concipi' (def. 1, I). Without *causa sui*, there is no power to conceive. This self-sufficiency of *causa sui* is God's freedom as principle of immanent causation. In nature, there is no transitive causality. God's unity is immanence.

On the basis of this divine unity, Spinoza rejects final cause. Final cause is the denial of the unity of God, an anthropomorphic and, thus, distorted reading of the plenitude of nature. God's perfection is absolute and immanent in each thing.

Plenum articulates as infinite things in infinite ways (prop. 16, I). God, the absolutely infinite, comprehends an infinity of perfections, of different ontic kinds, His attributes, each infinitely expressive of the divine essence. The absolute unity of God necessarily involves infinite attributes issuing in infinite modes, modes of every degree of power and perfection, from the infinite to the finite. Man is composed of finite modes of the attributes thought and extension, and the unity of the attributes is expressed in him as the epistemic union of mind and body. Body is the object of the mind, but this conception of body must be read in the context of man as enworlded being. Among the 'infinite things,' he is a one among many. Here, consciousness is perseverance against impingement, for durational being involves struggle for unification of the plurality of experience.

Spinoza's schema of the kinds of knowledge portrays human mind as a spectrum of unifications. We find that true knowledge involves unity of self in causal potency of adequation. The doctrine of *idea ideae* manifests the relation of consciousness to self-consciousness in the continuum of complexity that is the world of thought. Individuals represent differing degrees of complexity and consciousness. Just so, the individual may itself be characterized by differing degrees of active inseity. Certainty is the consumation of *idea ideae*. The true idea confirms itself, and mind knowing truly is not other than true idea. Thus, truth's affirmation of the active possession of its object in idea is also mind's self-possession in intrinsic causality. Adequate knowledge individuates, and, in certainty, the individual achieves its limit in essence.

Freedom is this ontic limit of the individual in essence. Spinoza rejects freedom of the will. In his dynamic determinism, freedom is actualization, of God in the transcendent actuality of eternity, of man in the conative actuality of duration. Even for the finite, identity is a power in a certain sense infinite. For Spinoza, the infinitude of the finite defines essence, and, in intuitive science, mind knows essence, achieving unimpeded participation in the continuum of creative act.

Yet, for durational man, essence is *conatus*. Transcendence is the struggle for transcendence. It is impossible that man not be a part of nature and that he conceive only adequate ideas. His existence does not follow from his essence, but is the many he continually seeks to unify in accordance with his meaning as individual. His form as power, empowered by participation in a transcendent whole, man's meaning is his mind as immanent intelligence of integration. Here, the ethical implications of the one and the many become evident. We see why Spinoza's account of unity and plurality must issue in an ethic. We understand the nature of good and evil.

The construction of the idea of man as moral exemplar involves valuation in terms of good and evil, a valuation that necessarily abstracts from the concrete perfection of being. How does this ideal man relate to the essence of man that is subject of the *Ethic*?

Our question requires thorough exploration of Spinoza's account of individuals and universals through clarification of the theory of common notions. Explicating Spinoza's conception of individual, we examine the relation of the attributes and infinite modes to the common properties, and of the common properties to the essences of finite individuals.

There emerge several possible answers to the question of the ontic status of the essence of man, a question that cannot be divorced from Spinoza's doctrine of immortality.

In conclusion, we take this doctrine of immortality as imperative to moral growth, suggesting Spinoza's special contribution to the realist rationalist tradition.

CHAPTER TWO

NATURA NATURANS AND *NATURA NATURATA*

Transformed by Spinoza's doctrine of God's immanence, the scholastic distinction between *natura naturans* and *natura naturata* becomes the expression of an infinite potency of continuity and differentiation.[1]

This terminology is introduced in the *Ethic* by the scholium to proposition 29, part I.

> Before I go any farther, I wish here to explain, or rather to recall to recollection, what we mean by *natura naturans* and what by *natura naturata*. For, from what has gone before, I think it is plain that by *natura naturans* we are to understand that which is in itself and is conceived through itself, or those attributes of substance which express eternal and infinite essence, that is to say . . . , God in so far as He is considered as a free cause. But by *natura naturata* I understand everything which follows from the necessity of the nature of God, or of any one of God's attributes, that is to say, all the modes of God's attributes in so far as they are considered as things which are in God, and which without God can neither be nor can be conceived.
>
> (schol. prop. 29, I)

> Antequam ulterius pergam, hic, quid nobis per Naturam naturantem, & quid per Naturam naturatam intelligendum sit, explicare volo, vel potius monere. Nam ex antecedentibus jam constare existimo, nempe, quod per Naturam naturantem nobis intelligendum est id, quod in se est, & per se concipitur, sive talia substantiae attributa, quae aeternam, & infinitam essentiam exprimunt, hoc est . . . , Deus, quatenus, ut causa libera, consideratur. Per naturatam autem intelligo id omne, quod ex necessitate Dei naturae, sive uniuscujusque Dei attributorum sequitur, hoc est, omnes Dei attributorum modos, quatenus considerantur, ut res, quae in Deo sunt, & quae sine Deo nec esse, nec concipi possunt.
>
> (II, 71, 5)

Thus, Spinoza distinguishes God from God's acts, distinguishes substance from its infinite modifications. Yet, this distinction posits a unity and does not evince a separation. God is as God's acts. 'From the necessity of the divine nature infinite numbers of things in infinite ways . . . must follow' (prop. 16, I). God or substance, in which all is and from which all must have its being, necessarily expresses itself as infinite individuals. Nothing is outside substance: God cannot be divided from His acts.

The scholium to proposition 29 differentiates *natura naturans* and *natura naturata* by the opposition of freedom and necessity, identifying creativity and the order of creation with freedom and necessity, respectively. Yet,

Spinoza has already demonstrated that, for a one beside whom there is no other, freedom is necessity (prop. 17, I), the necessity of an infinite internal complexity. God 'is compelled by no one' (prop. 17, I), but this does not imply an arbitrary freedom of will. The world does not come to be by divine fiat (props. 32 & 33 with dems., corols., schols., I). God's freedom is not a freedom of contingency, but of a plenitude of meaning, the infinite interdeterminations of an infinite power of forms of forms as divine idea. All things come to be 'which can be conceived by the infinite intellect' (prop. 16, I). God's freedom consists in being God.

We see emerging, in this discussion of freedom and necessity, the tension of unity and plurality, the tension of the one and the many.

For God, substance, freedom and necessity are one, because He is one, neither coerced by external others, nor fragmented and violated within by an alien being (1st additional proof of God's existence following prop. 11, I). Substance is consistent with itself.

Here, the relevance of Spinoza's doctrine of the indivisibility of substance comes to the fore as a basic interpretive principle in our account of *natura naturans* and *natura naturata*. In the immanentist teaching of Spinoza, the *naturans/naturata* distinction becomes an account of indivisibility and divisibility. It will be in this context that we find our key to Spinoza's conception of individuality and plurality, his doctrine of the one and the many.

'Substance absolutely infinite is indivisible' (prop. 13, I). In the scholium to proposition 13, part I, Spinoza posits the logical inter-changeability of the concepts of infinity and indivisibility. The infinite is, as it were, by definition, necessarily indivisible. The divisible is always the finite. God, as 'Being absolutely infinite' (def. 6, I), exists as the power of unity.[2]

While the theme of indivisible/divisible runs throughout the *Ethic*, perhaps its most succinct and explicit expression can be found in Spinoza's defense of God's corporeal or extended nature in the scholium to proposition 15, part I. We may take this discussion as emblematic.

Opponents of God's corporeality argue that God's infinite nature precludes extension. Starting from the premise that extension is com-posed of parts, they develop a series of paradoxes concerning lesser and greater infinites, and the additive generation of the infinite from the finite. These they employ as *reductio ad absurdum* arguments for God's incorporeality.

In this scholium, Spinoza demonstrates that the absurdity lies not in the assumption that extension is infinite, but in the assumption that extension is made up of discrete parts.

Calling upon those who deny the existence of a vacuum, he insists that parts really distinct cannot form a united whole. A discrete part, a kind of piece of reality, could be lifted away leaving a hole in being. Thus, a fully integrated real cannot be composed of separate parts.

This treatment of divine extension is rich in conclusions. From it, we learn that the absolute indivisibility of substance posits the absolute interrelatedness of any of its expressions. As perfect plenum of articulation, God issues as infinite continuum of being, of beings. Further, we learn that intellect necessarily conceives in unity. It is the nature of intellect to conceive the expressions of substance as continuous with one another and as unified in the whole that is their cause. Only imagination, in its abstract, superficial interpretation of substance, reads quantity as finite, divisible, composed of parts. This tells us that number and measure, for Spinoza, always refer to the imagination. Indeed, in his letter to Ludovicus Meyer on the nature of the infinite, in which the conclusions drawn from the scholium to proposition 15 are present in even greater detail, he describes number, measure, and also time as *auxilia imaginationis*, aids to the imagination.[3] To perceive reality as constituted by discrete parts, to make use of discrete, abstract units as mental tools is to be at the level of imagination. Number is not even adequate to geometrical space, e.g., a line does not consist of points.

Finally, from this scholium, we also realize the dependence of this imaginative division on the authentic 'divisibility' of substance, i.e., its infinite power to generate infinite things in infinite ways (prop. 16, I). Division is parasitical upon differentiation. The modes are parts of substance, but their differentiation, their individuality, is genetically derived from an infinite complex of community of essence. This community of essence, that of the *propria communia*, the common properties, will occupy us much in later chapters.

Natura naturans and *natura naturata* are, then, God or substance as indivisible and as infinitely divisible, in the sense just defined. For Spinoza, the one must be many and the many must be one.

CHAPTER THREE

ETERNITY AS THE EXISTENCE OF GOD
AND THE DERIVATION OF DURATION

Failure to grasp the meaning of eternity in the *Ethic* will vitiate the entire work. Spinoza's conception of eternity is, quite literally, the substance of the *Ethic*.

In the concluding definition of the *Ethic*, part I, Spinoza writes:

> By eternity, I understand existence itself, so far as it is conceived necessarily to follow from the definition alone of the external thing. Explanation.—For such existence, like the essence of the thing, is conceived as an eternal truth. It cannot therefore be explained by duration or time, even if the duration be conceived without beginning or end. (def. 8, I)

> Per aeternitatem intelligo ipsam existentiam, quatenus ex sola rei aeternae definitione necessario sequi concipitur. Explicatio.—Talis enim existentia, ut aeterna veritas, sicut rei essentia, concipitur, propterea que per durationem, aut tempus explicari non potest, tametsi duratio principio, & fine carere concipiatur. (II, 46, 13)

We read here what might appear a merely logical account of eternity. Spinoza writes of definition and of logical entailment, seemingly of abstract principles. Indeed, only from the vantage point of intuitive science in part V, does the conception of eternity receive full content, do we understand that, in this definition, Spinoza addresses the being of being itself.

Nevertheless, by the end of part I, eternity has been identified with *causa sui*: the eternal thing is a unique and infinite power of being (dem. prop. 7 & dem. prop. 34, I). We know that Spinoza is not talking about an abstract logical principle, but about the concrete individual that is source and ground of everything real. Definition itself, then, we must conclude, has ontological and not merely logical status. The order of thought grounds in the order of being, and to define anything is to grasp its meaning as being, thus, for Spinoza, to know it through its cause.

It is through the meaning of eternity that Spinoza demonstrates the necessary unity of God's essence and existence. God as self-generating substance necessarily exists, i.e., His existence follows by definition from the meaning of substance (props. 7 & 11, I). He is thus eternal (prop. 19, I). The attributes express the essence of substance: they define God. Forms of divine essence, they are eternal by God's eternity, expressive of His infinite ontic power, power of infinite existence. The attributes, then, manifest both divine essence and divine existence, and at once constitutive of each, posit their identity (prop. 20 with dem., I).

It is interesting and instructive to apply the definition of essence offered in part II to the divine nature.

> I say that to the essence of anything pertains that, which being given, the thing itself is necessarily posited, and being taken away, the thing is necessarily taken; or, in other words, that without which the thing can neither be nor be conceived, and which in its turn cannot be nor be conceived without the thing.   (def. 2, II)

> Ad essentiam alicujus rei id pertinere dico, quo dato res necessario ponitur, & quo sublato res necessario tollitur; vel id, sine quo res, & vice versa quod sine re nec esse, nec concipi potest.   (II, 84, 17)

Spinoza makes explicit his intention to distinguish individual things from God by this definition (dem. prop. 10, II). Discussing a traditional definition of essence as 'that without which the thing can neither be nor be conceived,' he emphasizes his addition of 'that which in its turn cannot be nor be conceived without the thing' (schol. corol. prop. 10, II). For Spinoza, nothing can be conceived apart from God. God's essence is the universal source of being.[4] It does not, however, constitute the essence of individual things. Individuals are not identical with God. Note that, by the same stroke, Spinoza differentiates God from finite individuals, and the essence from the existence of the finite individual. The way in which the finite is othered from God bears an intimate logical relationship to the difference between essence and existence in that finite being. 'The essence of things produced by God does not involve existence' (prop. 24, I).

Here, we observe that this definition, designed to address the relation of essence to existence in the finite being, can be applied with full consistency to absolutely infinite being. Such application does not violate the definition, rather we find in God's perfect reciprocity of essence and existence the archetype of the definition's fulfillment.

Again and again, Spinoza's network of concepts leads us back to unity. Substance must exist (prop. 7, I) and therefore must be one (prop. 14, I). What is one inviolably must exist (props. 12 & 13; schol. prop. 15, I).

While *natura naturans/natura naturata* cannot be identified with God's essence and existence, the latter unity may correctly be understood as the 'possibility' of the former. The divine essence and existence are one. Thus, at the furthest reach of nature, substance cannot be alienated from itself. God creates infinitely without being othered.

Spinoza terms God's essence and existence eternal truths (corol. 1 prop. 20, I). The logical structure of the *Ethic*, with its insistence upon the role of intellect in knowing nature as timeless order of necessity, may well suggest that 'eternal truth' is some type of universal axiom. As our discussion of reason and intuitive science will show, this interpretation of 'eternal truth' is not false, but insufficient. This misinterpretation of 'eternal truth' leads to the misinterpretation of God's eternity. We have suggested that the eternity of God is not a timeless network of logical entailment, or rather not merely such a network, but being fully realized and concrete. The laws of nature are abstractions from the infinite meaning of nature itself. Axioms of interaction, these laws are abstracted from the concrete being of substance, and describe the dynamic, generative divine necessity more in logical than ontological terms.

Eternity, then, is not a logico-mathematical necessity void of vital being, but the realization and consumation of what we know as life. Eternity, for Spinoza, is not the privation of duration. Duration is the privation of eternity.[5] God's nature must stand first in the order of knowledge (schol. corol. prop. 10, II), and from it the nature of finite things be derived, so from eternity must be derived the experience of living things.

For Spinoza, eternity contains duration. Duration is not illusion, but no more is eternity abstraction. The 'eternal truth' of divine essence and existence is the truth of duration, the truth about duration. The endurance of the enduring springs from eternity. The power by which each thing perseveres is the power of God, conditioned and again conditioned by infinite other expressions of that power, but existent only as continuous with the whole (prop. 9, II), as following from God, 'to whose nature alone existence pertains' (corol. prop. 24, I).

As our discussion of *conatus* will make clear, duration is a function of individuals. God's eternity is infinite act, so likewise is duration the activity of finite individuals. We note three points in the derivation of duration. First, duration expresses the immanence of God in the finite individual. Second, duration derives from the unity of God as interrelation of all beings. Third, duration reflects the partiality of the finite being as partial expression of the whole.

The force of continuance that is the life of the finite involves no internal limit (expl. def. 5, II & prop. 8, III). Duration emerges as quality of being. The actuality of a finite individual is actualization of eternal potency in enjoyment of essence (prop. 7 & schol. prop. 57, III).

This actualization arrives in the context of a causal complex. The finite individual acts in reaction to infinite other finitudes. That which follows from the absolute nature of God is necessarily infinite and eternal (props. 21 & 22, I). Finite, durational being demands determination by the finite and durational. It is and acts under the impact of other and yet other finitudes to infinity (prop. 28, I). In inviolable unity, the laws of the divine nature comprehend even the furthest finitude (schol. prop. 28 & appendix, I).

Within a nexus of finite causes, each endures, and this qualitative duration, or experience, may be conceived abstractly as a kind of quantity to which temporal measure may be applied. Time, however, is only an aid to imagination, incommensurable with the order of the real. The possibility of time, number, measure, itself derives from abstract comparison of concrete expressions of substance. It is because all things are interrelated in the plenum of nature that one may select a motion as measure of other motions.

Finally, that each part of nature is of itself a whole affects the relation of part to part. We find partiality not merely as integrated difference, but as bias. In its tendency to refer its other to self, the finite being echos the self-sufficient unity of infinite being, but, for the part, this tendency distorts its true relation to its complement in nature. The finite being imagines the world, not in the sense that the world of duration is illusion, but in the sense that imagination's privative reading of the real is duration. Things are referred to self, rather than to God. The emendation of this displacement by an ordering of intellect is realized in the eternity of the human mind.

In the latter propositions of part I, Spinoza descends through the infinite immediate and mediate modes (props. 21 & 22, I) to portray the existence of the finite mode. The necessity of the divine nature becomes the necessary determination of the finite mode (props. 26-29, I). We move from the being of substance to the becoming of the modes.

For Spinoza, there is change without contingency.

> In nature there is nothing contingent, but all things are determined from the necessity of the divine nature to exist and act in a certain manner.
> (prop. 29, I)

> In rerum natura nullum datur contingens, sed omnia ex necessitate divinae naturae determinata sunt ad certo modo existendum, & operandum.
> (II, 70, 17)

The flux of duration does not randomly befall the mode, though the fragmented and partial perception of the finite being reads its life as change and chance, experiences duration as contingency. Yet, it is not a case of things happening in order, of a temporal ordering transcending durational consciousness. The determinism that makes natural science possible, even a rational natural science, is only the surface of the deep intelligibility of the whole. The absence of any true contingency at the level of time does not tell the full force of God's immutability (corol 2, prop. 20, I). Eternity is the being of God, the realization of his changelessness.

> It cannot . . . be explained by duration or time, even if the duration be conceived without beginning or end. (explan. def, 8, I)

> per durationem, aut tempus explicari non potest, tametsi duratio principio, & fine carere concipiatur. (II, 46, 18)

CHAPTER FOUR

CAUSA SUI:
DIVINE CAUSALITY
AS FREEDOM AND DETERMINISM

In the *Ethic*, Spinoza does not explicitly discuss the role of causality in definition.[6] This role reveals itself through the interrelated concepts of knowledge and definition. The nature of a thing is known through its cause (axiom 4, I & def. 1, III). Causal identity defines a thing. Definition expresses of any thing its nature or essence. 'The true definition of any one thing neither involves nor expresses anything except the nature of the thing defined' (schol. 2 prop. 8, I). Definition concerns essence. Thus, the cause for the existence of anything less than the whole is not contained in the definition of the thing itself (schol. 2 prop. 8, I).

As we have seen, there is, and can be, only one thing from whose definition existence follows. Substance cannot be produced by any other substance (corol. prop. 6, I). Hence, it must be cause of itself, *causa sui*. Its essence must involve existence. From this internal necessity of existence follows infinitude (prop. 8, I), the range of qualitative infinitude to be gathered up into the absolutely infinite nature of God (schol. prop. 10, I). The being of being absolutely infinite follows by definition.

> God, or substance consisting of infinite attributes, each one of which expresses eternal and infinite essence, necessarily exists.   (prop. 11, I)

> Deus, sive substantia constans infinitis attributis, quorum unumquodque aeternam, & infinitam essentiam exprimit, necessario existit. (II, 52, 23)

This proposition with its demonstration offers in brief the ontological argument of the *Ethic* in its entirety. The *Ethic* is the ontological argument.

The ontological argument of proposition 11 is not the logical derivation of a property from an abstract conception of God. Though the full content of the idea of God requires the *Ethic* as a whole, even here, Spinoza claims by the nature of infinite being the necessity of our idea. He shows that our idea necessarily follows from the necessity of being, not that the logical requirements of thought, as it were, compel God to exist. Logical necessity derives from the divine nature. What God is absolutely conditions what we can know of Him. It is by the power of the self-caused that we define Him as potency to be Himself.

In this context, our claim that the entire *Ethic* is an ontological argument reiterates a central point about God's essence. God's essence has an infinitely complex structure. The possibility of defining God derives directly from His status as *causi sui*. He is what Spinoza calls the 'internal proximate cause' of Himself.[7] Only the complex can be understood through its cause, the simple must be grasped directly.[8]

The complexity of God is an inexhaustible complexity. God cannot exhaust His creativity. All things conceived by the infinite intellect necessarily exist (prop. 16, I). God does not withhold being from anything, no more could he choose not to be God. One, infinitely othering, He cannot be drained of the potency to understand, the potency to be. This potency, indeed, cannot be bifurcated. God does not think of things He does not do. Those who claim that an infinite creativity would exhaust God's power to be deny and do not affirm His omnipotence (schol. prop. 17, I).

Then, infinite things in infinite ways follow from the necessity of God's nature. Infinite essence involves infinite properties. From the definition of infinite essence infinite properties may be inferred (dem. prop. 16, I). Further, the laws by which all things are brought to being express the complex internal structure of that infinite essence. Being constructs its properties by integral potency as ground. God's causal efficacy is primal and purely intrinsic.

In God, 'the necessity of the divine nature' is not constraint, but explication of essence. Nothing compels God to act (prop. 17, I). All things are in God and conceived through Him. There is no other to compel Him. This purely internal necessity of the divine causality is God's freedom. 'He acts from the necessity alone of His own nature. . . . Therefore . . . He alone is a free cause' (corol. 2 prop. 17, I). We see that Spinoza identifies freedom with the internal necessity of self-expression, of internally determined activity. God's status as singular being vouch-safes this potency of infinite self-expression, this infinitely actualized self-interpretation. Freedom is unimpeded causal efficacy.

From the absolute oneness of God's nature, we conclude His freedom as first and efficient cause of all things (corol. 1 & corol. 3 prop. 16, I). From the absolute oneness of God's nature, we conclude His freedom as cause through Himself: He causes because of Himself and is the being of that because (corol. 2 prop. 16, I). Thus:

> God is the immanent, and not the transitive cause of all things. (prop. 18, I)

> Deus est omnium rerum causa immanens, non vero transiens. (II, 63, 33)

This is truly a pivotal proposition in the *Ethic*. In it Spinoza lays down the rule of generation. Unity flows from unity. The power of each to be itself issues from God's power to be God. As we move, in the latter propositions of book I, to the determinate existence of particulars, we must recall this principle. Finitude demands finitude (prop. 28, I), but the power by which each thing persists derives directly from God. The existence of the finite being does not follow necesarily from its essence (axiom 1, II), but that being, both as essence and as existence, necessarily has God as its efficient cause (prop. 25, I). The unconditioned activity of God or nature generates the interactions of nature. A thing is conditioned, acted upon, determined, in so far as it acts. This is not, of course, the action of the morally free individual of part V, but rather action as the power of passivity. These are not Spinoza's words. Yet, we void his account of finitude, if we do not grasp the immanence of God in all things as activity. God is not outside anything, just as He is not outside Himself.

God or nature is one, a continuum, in which all things are interrelated, and they are interrelated through what they intrinsically are. Thus are the powers of specific essence the forms of genesis. The interdetermination of all the modes of substance flows from the complex activity of each individual as infinitely integrated into an infinite real. Even external impingement expresses only the nature of those things involved. In the absolute sense, there is no transitive causality.

Passing outward from attribute through immediate and mediate infinite modes into the finite modes, Spinoza names the ranges of causality and causal activity that define nature. The power of God is the energy by which each thing means itself, for the meaning of any thing is the essential power of its self-expression, its identity in action. A thing is determinate in its essence. It is what God makes it to be. Further, its existence is determinate by the interdetermination of all things. The interrelation of all things in the continuum of the divine nature is their necessary determination one of the other.[9]

The individual, experiencing in the 'common order of nature,' finds both contingency and transitive causality. Chance and empirical science are phenomena of the privation of wholeness. In the perspective of the whole, determinism names the self-defining nature of divinity. The necessity of our being as finite individuals is the freedom of God, and, as we shall see, precisely in this necessity is also our freedom.

CHAPTER FIVE

ONTOLOGICAL FULLNESS OF BEING AND THE DENIAL OF FINAL CAUSE: THE MEANING OF PERFECTION

The dynamic plenum of substance generates infinite modes in infinite ways. These affections of the divine nature follow of necessity the rule of plenum: everything determines everything else. The creativity of God, absolute and constitutive, manifests a whole of fully determinate parts. The existence and activity of any individual mode or part of nature arises not from some contingent freedom, but from the sure order of its place in nature.

This divine fullness of being grounds Spinoza's critique of final cause. We shall see that the notion of final cause inherently denies the unity of God, a unity that is absolute.

In the *Ethic*, we find two major treatments of the rejection of final cause, the first in the appendix to part I, the second in the preface to part IV. This latter discussion relates to the examination of transcendental and universal notions offered in the first scholium to the proposition 40, part II.

Spinoza's unrelenting account of God's omnipotence in the *Ethic*, part I, leads in the appendix to a total rejection of an anthropomorphizing reading of nature. Man is not the measure of all things.

The anthropomorphic conception of nature interprets God's 'motives' in creation on the analogy of man's, that is, man projects his ignorance about the causal nature of his own activity onto the whole. Man's desire is determined by external causes, but, unconscious of this, while conscious of the desire itself, he believes that he is free and freely seeks that which he desires. The object of desire, what man judges useful in its satisfaction, he regards as the end of his seeking. He understands all activities in terms of ends or final causes. In ignorance of the causal order of nature, as of his own causal determination, and, finding in nature much profitable to him, man assumes that some god or gods have created all nature for his use. Thus, he endeavours to discover the final causes of all things, the profitability of nature being proof of man's importance. Spinoza writes:

> This attempt, however, to show that nature does nothing in vain (that is to say, nothing which is not profitable to man), seems to end in showing that nature, the gods, and man are alike mad. (appendix, I)

> Sed dum quaesiverunt ostendere, naturam nihil frustra (hoc est, quod in usum hominum non sit) agere, nihil aliud videntur ostendisse, quam naturam, Deosque aeque, ac homines delirare.   (II, 79, 15)

Much in nature is beneficial to man, but much is injurious. Man, in order that he maintain his sense of centrality, interprets the injurious as punishment by the gods for wrongs inflicted them or faults in the manner of man's worship, but, as such punishment appears to fall to just and unjust alike, man is forced to conclude that the judgement of the gods surpasses his comprehension.

In the face of the multiplex and various effects of nature, man holds tenaciously to his own imagined significance, accounting most important that in nature which affects him most beneficially. According as a thing pleases the human body, man judges it good. According as a thing pains the body, man judges it evil. Then, from this judgement of all things in terms of bodily affect, come such notions as good, evil, order, confusion, beauty, and deformity. It is, thus, at the level of imagination, that man forms his concepts for interpreting nature. The 'order' of nature is the facility of the imagination, and confusion, its overwhelming by the plenum. Beauty is physical pleasure the body takes in some part of nature, deformity, the body's discomfort.

The body's enhancement as interpretive principle ties to the anthropocentric understanding of divine nature already described. The gods create in order that they may be held in honor, reward and punish according to inscrutable judgement. If men judge good and evil that which conduces or does not conduce to their well-being, then they must so judge that which conduces or does not conduce to the worship of gods in whose power that well-being lies.

These powerful and primitive superstitions bind men into the imaginal life of the 'human fictions' of end or final cause. Spinoza writes of the development of mathematics, 'which does not deal with ends, but with the essences and properties of forms' (appendix, I), as major breakthrough for the transcendence of imagination by intellect. Setting before man 'another rule of truth,' it begins to turn him to the rational study of nature.

Rational men require no theodicy. God is perfect, infinite essence, perfect power. There is no evil, ugliness, confusion to account for.

> For the perfection of things is to be judged by their nature and power alone; nor are they more or less perfect because they delight or offend the human senses, or because they are beneficial or prejudicial to human nature.
> (appendix, I)

Nam rerum perfectio ex sola earum natura, & potentia est aestimanda, nec ideo res magis, aut minus perfectae sunt, propterea quod hominum sensum delectant, vel offendunt, quod humanae naturae conducunt, vel quod eidem repugnant.   (II, 83, 22)

We note here that from the perfection of God, the perfection of each thing follows. In and of itself, each thing is perfect. Only through comparison of different individuals do we acquire the idea of the imperfect. God's immanence is an immanence of perfection. Each thing is with the being of God, and the being of God, with which it is, is internal to it. The unity and uniqueness of each thing flows from the unity of God.

The function of comparison in the application of final cause and its role in the employment of universal ideas, Spinoza takes up in the preface to part IV. By this discussion, our understanding of Spinoza's conception of God's perfection will also be further clarified.

In the appendix to part I, Spinoza has referred to the desires out of which men act, seeking what is useful or advantageous to them. This utility to desire is the end for which they act.

When man, having consciously sought an end, achieves it, he considers his deed accomplished. From this, Spinoza argues in part IV, first arise notions of perfection and imperfection. The perfect is the accomplished. In the Latin of the original text, the basis of the conjoining of these concepts is immediately evident, for *perficere* means 'to accomplish.' 'Perfect' and 'accomplished' are expressed by the same word. In terms of the intention of its author, a deed was first judged perfect or imperfect.

This notion of perfection was then assimilated to that of the universal or type. Men thought about the types of things they could make and came to prefer some types to others, each man judging his preferred type the model to which others of its kind should be compared. Men came to judge perfect or imperfect those things that best approximated or failed to approximate the universals or types they had conceived. Generalizing from artifical objects, they judged natural things also by universal ideas they had formed of them. In the belief that nature acted, as they did, to achieve some end, they regarded these universals as the models of creation. Anything not answering to this man-made model, men described as imperfect, concluding that in it nature had failed or made a mistake. This judgement on the ends or goals of nature through the comparison of particulars to universal ideas represents imaginal thinking about nature.

In the first scholium to proposition 40, part II, Spinoza has laid down the physiological basis of the universal idea drawn upon in the preface to part IV. He rejects the universals and transcendentals posited by

scholastic philosophy as confused aggregates of images. Species definitions and abstract genera so derived possess no validity for a rational
science of nature.[10]

Yet, in the preface, Spinoza presses even further than this the
limitations of perfection and imperfection as universal terms.

> Perfection . . . and imperfection are really only modes of thought; that is to
> say, notions which we are in the habit of forming from the comparison with
> one another of individuals of the same species or genus, and this is the
> reason why I have said . . . that by reality and perfection I understand the
> same thing; for we are in the habit of referring all individuals in nature to
> one genus, which is the most general; that is to say, to the notion of being,
> which embraces absolutely all the individual objects in nature. In so far,
> therefore, as we refer the individual objects in nature to this genus, and
> compare them one with another, and discover that some possess more being
> or reality than others, in so far do we call some more perfect than others.
>
> (preface, IV)

> Perfectio . . . & imperfectio revera modi solummodo cogitandi sunt, nempe
> notiones, quas fingere solemus ex eo, quod ejusdem speciei, aut generis
> individua ad invicem comparamus: & hac de causa supra . . . dixi me per
> realitatem, & perfectionem idem intelligere; solemus enim omnia Naturae
> individua ad unum genus, quod generalissimum appellatur, revocare;
> nempe ad notionem entis, quae ad omnia absolute Naturae individua
> pertinet. Quatenus itaque Naturae individua ad hoc genus revocamus, & ad
> invicem comparamus, & alia plus entitatis, seu realitatis, quam alia habere
> comperimus, eatenus alia aliis perfectiora esse dicimus.   (II, 207, 18)

This claim we have tried to express by describing each and every thing in
nature as perfect. Spinoza puts forth a kind of ontological equity of all
things. The absolute plenitude and immanence of divine perfection voids
the term: where in perfect unity perfection is all, comparison is
meaningless.

No universal can express the concrete individuality of substance. In
the preface, Spinoza is not only speaking about the universals generated
by imagination, but also about the universals of reason. In the second
scholium to proposition 40, part II, Spinoza identifies the various ways
in which the mind forms universal ideas. Universal ideas formed from
sense perception of individual things and from signs, he refers to
imagination, but there are also rational universals, epistemically valid
universals grounded in the common properties of things. We believe
that, in the preface to part IV, Spinoza delimits the conceptual reach of
these rational universals, as well as rejecting the cognitive efficacy of
universals formed in the imagination.[11]

Spinoza does speak of God's perfection and does compare the perfection of one thing with another. His definition of perfection, however,

gives the control with reference to which this conception must be interpreted.

> By reality and perfection I understand the same thing. (def. 6, II)

> Per realitatem, & perfectionem idem intelligo. (II, 85, 15)

Thus, throughout the *Ethic*, we must always read perfection in the terms of a tension between its concrete and rationally abstract meanings. Drawn between the possibility and the impossibility of comparison that ground in the immanent differentiation and the indivisibility of substance, the appellation 'perfect' must always counter itself. Some things express greater reality. We can call these more perfect. Yet, perfection as the concrete being of substance cannot be abstracted away from itself. God is one (corol. 1 prop. 14, I).

Here, we confront a prime principle in our interpretation of the *Ethic*. Every denomination of God, 'perfect,' 'whole,' 'one,' that is not the affection of an attribute must be taken through this tension of concrete/ abstract.[12] The concrete reality of substance pulls against the language of the text, even in its capacity to denote rational universals.

Stressing the concrete, unique reality of substance as absolutely infinite individual and the concrete, unique reality of every individual following therefrom, Spinoza denies any ontic status to final cause. Everything is itself, therefore, perfect. No comparison can be made.

All is perfect because perfection comes first in the order of being, and here we may validly speak of a hierarchy of perfection, though keeping ever in mind the indivisible unity of God extending to being possessed of the least measure of being. Everything is in God, but what is 'furthest' from him remains less perfect than the 'nearest,' that which follows directly from the divine nature (props. 21–23 with dems., I) Final cause, thus, reverses the order of nature by making the 'furthest' the end for which God acts, the most perfect (appendix, I). In the genuine hierarchy of nature, what is closest to God is the most comprehensive expression of being.

God, then, does not act purposively, with an end in view, but creates from the necessity of His own nature. Creation, the infinite and eternal divine creativity, is not made to the measure of man. That which serves our purpose, serves always its own purpose, as also the purpose of infinite other things. This principle is central to the ethical import of Spinoza's doctrine: everything in nature has infinite functions.

CHAPTER SIX

THE MULTIPLICITY OF GOD AND
THE MULTIPLICITY OF SENSE

> By God, I understand Being absolutely infinite, that is to say, substance consisting of infinite attributes, each one of which expresses eternal and infinite essence.
>
> (def. 6, I)

> Per Deum intelligo ens absolute infinitum, hoc est, substantiam constantem infinitis attributis, quorum unumquodque aeternam, & infinitam essentiam exprimit.
>
> (II, 45, 22)

The absolute unity of being must involve an essence of unnumbered aspect, an infinity of attributes. The inviolably one achieves its limit as the absolutely infinite. Each attribute is infinite in its own kind, and God consists in infinite kinds.

Attribute is the form through which intellect knows the essence of substance (def. 4, I), and each, as irreducible expression of sole substance, must necessarily be known through itself (prop. 10, I). The attributes are genuine powers of substance. In knowing them, the intellect knows truly. For Spinoza, to know essence is to know truly, and in the attributes intellect knows the essence of God.[13]

Spinoza, in book I, introduces the notion of attribute as abstract principle of a kind of being. To God pertain infinite kinds of being. Only in book II, does attribute become concrete for us with the proofs of thought and extension as divine attributes.

> Thought is an attribute of God, or God is a thinking thing.   (prop. 1, II)

> Extension is an attribute of God, or God is an extended thing. (prop. 2, II)

> Cogitatio attributum Dei est, sive Deus est res cogitans.   (II, 86, 11)

> Extension attributum Dei est, sive Deus est res extensa.   (II, 86, 30)

All individual things are finite modes of God's attributes (corol. prop. 25, I), but bodies and ideas, the determinate expressions of God as extended and thinking thing (defs. 1 & 3, II) alone are felt or perceived by human beings (axiom 5, II). Of infinite attributes, we know only thought and extension, for the essence of man consists of modifications of these two attributes (corol. prop. 10, II). God's being issues as the determinate being of man, and through this being, the thinking, extended being of ourselves, do we know God.

We have seen that the infinity of attributes expresses one, sole being. Their diversity is inseparable from their unity. In the case of human being, being constituted merely by thought and extension, this unity of the attributes of substance manifests as the epistemic union of mind and body.

This epistemic union has ontological status, as Spinoza's epistemology is itself ontological claim concerning divine unity and complexity. We argue that it is precisely in terms of idea and ideate that Spinoza works to explicate the identity and difference of the attributes.

The paradigm of this union is the idea of God, God's idea of His attributes and modes. This divine understanding or intelligence is as *causa sui*, the integral expression of the attribute thought. It is self-generating and not caused by its object (prop. 5, II). Ideas involve the conception of thought and must be understood through thought alone (dem. prop. 5, II). Just so, each mode of substance must be conceived through the attribute of which it is a modification (prop. 6 with dem. II).

This dependence of mode on attribute represents the causal integrity of attribute. A thing is and is conceived through the attribute of which it is affection: that attribute is its cause (prop. 6, II). Here, the identity of attributes gives us the parallelism of causal orders.

> The order and connection of ideas is the same as the order and connection of things.   (prop. 7, II)

> Ordo, & connexio idearum idem est, ac ordo, & connexio rerum.
> (II, 89, 21)

The totality of nature as pattern of infinite causal interaction can be read as thought or as extension, and the place of any determinate thing within the nexus be read as mind or body (schol. prop. 7, II).

We have spoken of the attribute as the cause of its modifications. This is absolutely so. All things are in and are conceived through God. The finite thing, however, takes on being within the conditioned causality of infinite interdeterminations.

> The idea of an individual thing actually existing has God for a cause, not in so far as He is infinite, but in so far as He is considered to be affected by another idea of an individual thing actually existing, of which idea also He is the cause in so far as He is affected by a third, and so on *ad infinitum*.
> (prop. 9, II)

> Idea rei singularis, actu existentis, Deum pro causa habet, non quatenus infinitus est, sed quatenus alia rei singularis actu existentis idea affectus consideratur, cujus etiam Deus est causa, quatenus alia tertia affectus est, & sic in infinitum.   (II, 91, 30)

This means that God knows the finite thing as worlded. His idea of any object involves the causal field of its articulation (corol. & dem. prop. 9, II). It is a one among many. Thus, man by essence stands a one among many, a finite power in the tension of the whole. His is not an immutable, necessary existence, but an existence of durational flux. He must live the transformations that the whole decrees (prop. 10 with dem., II & prop. 4 with dem., IV). We know already from proposition 9, part II, and its corollary that these transformations will not be fully understood through the essence of him in transformation.

Man does not know himself as infinite, necessary being (dem. prop. 11, II), but as actually existing individual. In the context of the book II account of finitude, actual existence clearly refers to determination of time and place, the existential rather than essential actuality of man (schol. prop. 29, V). To speak of time and place is, however, already to abstract from the quality of existence Spinoza seeks to describe. Time and place are abstractions from the relations of actually existing things. Spinoza shows the object of the idea forming the actual being of the human mind to be the worlded body (props. 11 & 13, II). Indeed, he shall show the affected body as the world of the actual individual (axiom 4, II).

The idea of God is the mind of the world as transformational totality, and integrates the individual minds of infinite finite beings. Divine intellect issues as this complex of consciousness, and the mind of each being partakes in thought as 'a part of the infinite intellect of God' (corol. prop. 11, II).

Here lies the basis of Spinoza's philosophy of experience and epistemic transcendence. The human mind necessarily perceives all that befalls the body (prop. 12, II), but it cannot understand all that befalls the body. God manifests the essence of human mind as the individual's awareness of itself, but His idea of this individual involves ideas of those others with which it interacts. The individual knows itself partially or inadequately (corol. prop. 11, II). For Spinoza, events, the befallings, cannot be understood but as abstractions from individual agency. For every individual, its experience is *its* experience. Even in its confused and privative reading of its transcendence by the whole, the individual unknowingly knows. It remains to show how this doctrine of immanence and encounter applies to the specific complexity of the human organism.

We have noted that the epistemic union of mind and body precludes causal interaction. Mind does not determine body, and body does not determine mind (prop. 2, III), rather, mind is the knowing of body. For Spinoza, the universality and immanence of God's thought renders all nature animate (schol. prop. 13, II). That the causal order of thought must parallel that of extension does not mean, however, that mind directly impinges upon mind. This would undercut the tension of subject and object that is the basis of the mind's ability to understand.

Spinoza maintains with great rigor the continuity of consciousness. All things are animate as affections of God as potency of thought. For Spinoza, no physicality is without mental counterpart. Reality is conscious, that is, minded, which is not to claim for other species or kinds of being a consciousness properly only human. Indeed, the ensoulment of all matter does not of itself posit minds, for example, for minerals. Mind is consciousness as immanence (corol. prop. 9, II), thus, it is in so far as a thing is an individual that it is minded. We may speak of cats and cows as individual in some meaningful sense. The soul status of rocks or even viruses is rendered impossible of judgement by the problems of here applying criteria of individuation. For Spinoza, stone is minded, but that need not mean a pebble has a soul. The import of Spinoza's claim for the continuity of consciousness comes to the fore, rather, in man's participation in divine intelligence and in the relation of human mind to human mind. Minds are related to one another: in a radical sense, ideas can be shared.

Yet, the mind of one thing is presented to another not subjectively but objectively. Our experience of the psychical power of another is not independent of the mediation of body. Mind presents as thing, and through our body and mind we come to grasp the thing as mind. We might say that the individual experiences every other individual directly indirectly. Thus does other as object of encounter relate to the body of percipient self, body as other.

The unity and diversity of the attributes finds expression in the tension subject/object, mind and body as idea and ideate (props. 11–29, II). Body does not cut off mind from mind because body is not mind, but, further, body does not cut off mind from mind because body is mind (prop. 10, I; prop. 6, schol. prop. 7, II; prop. 2, III). Mind and body are other and one, and the nature of their union, their unity, is the necessary organization of consciousness in terms of an object (axiom 3, II).

The objects of those ideas that are the minds of finite things may differ from one another in excellence of being. So likewise, their ideas will differ. Spinoza defines this excellence as breadth of experience and potency of differentiation. The body's ability 'to do or suffer many things' (schol. prop. 13, II) and to act in self-sufficient manner corresponds to the mind's ability to perceive many things and to distinctly understand. Here lies the superiority of the complex organism, the superiority of man and of the mind of man to grasp the real. The more world the body embodies, the greater is its power to differentiate itself from its complement in nature, the other of the world that transcends it.

The indivisible essence of substance extended, modified by the eternal infinite immediate mode of motion and rest, finds determination in the constellation of infinite finitudes, the infinite mediate mode that is called in letter 64 the *facies totius universi*, the fashion or make of the whole universe.[14] This is the transcendent transformational body of God, in which other has been subsumed without sublation. All things are transcended by the whole, which in uniting transcends them.

We may speak of the *corpora simplicissima*, the simplest bodies, as living at the edge of creation, but this is metaphor. Spinoza's God has no edge. Beyond being non-being is not. The simplest bodies have their being at the heart of being. God is not the 'remote cause' of any singular (schol. prop. 28, I). The interaction of the *corpora simplicissima* according to necessary kinetic laws generates more complex bodies (discursus on body following prop. 13, II). The simplest bodies are separable only by abstraction from the complexes that they constitute.[15]

These more complex bodies are defined by a certain fixed proportion of motion and rest (def. in discursus on body, II). The form of an individual is this proportionate union of bodies (dem. lem. 4, discursus on body, II). Its identity depends not upon the matter composing it, but upon the maintenance of structure.[16] Spinoza accounts for the transformational potential of the individual, its power to change while retaining bodily integrity.[17] Further, he shows us how higher and yet higher order individuals mesh to form an immutable mutable individual: nature as a whole of constantly changing parts. Spinoza permits us to view from either end 'the make of the universe,' deduced from the absolute nature of God as infinite mediate mode issuing from motion and rest, and constructed from the *corpora simplicissima*, as union of unions into the equipoise and fruition of an infinite whole (prop. 22, I & schol. lem. 7, discursus on body, II).

In the discursus on the nature of body, Spinoza locates man within this continuum of most simple to most complex.

> The human body is composed of a number of individuals of diverse nature, each of which is composite to a high degree. (post. 1, discursus on body, II)

> Corpus humanum componitur ex plurimis (diversae naturae) individuis, quorum unumquodque valde compositum est.   (II, 102, 20)

The human body is worlded body, complex individual embodied within infinitely complex individual. Man requires world for nourishment, the empowerment of change as identity (post. 4, discursus, II), and himself possesses potency to change the world by affecting other bodies (post. 6, discursus, II). Moreover, his composition in terms of hard, soft, and fluid parts portrays the combination of resistance and responsiveness making experience possible (posts. 2, 3, & 5, discursus, II). We cannot speak of 'experience' where there is absolute fluidity, absolute rigidity. The body retains its identity under impingement, but responds to the others acting upon it. The body holds its own in the flux of matter, feeding upon the circumambient world and acting in it. Likewise, we shall find the human mind defined by openness to affection and intrinsic potency for clarification, that power of breadth and differentiation of which we have spoken.

Thus, human mind 'begins' as awareness of a 'certain body affected in many ways' (axiom 4, II). Nevertheless, we would radically misunderstand Spinoza, should we identify the nature of body with the body we perceive.

> The human body exists as we perceive it.   (corol. prop. 13, II)

> . . . sequitur . . . Corpus humanum, prout ipsum sentimus, existere.
>   (II, 96, 19)

The human body is as we perceive it, but perception does not yield whole the body to our understanding. What the body is can be realized only by intellect in the transcendence of sense. From this perspective, Spinoza gives us body as world of the embodied individual.

We remember that, for Spinoza, God is unconditioned activity, the finite individual, conditioned activity. All being is agency. Thus is the 'body' of the *Ethic* body in act, body as a potency of reagency, reacting to its active complement in nature, power of response delimited by the measure of qualitative community. The more complex articulates itself in terms of other by means of shared qualities of being. The organism defines itself in the continuum of being: the work of creation, of divine activity, continues in the finite individual. Infinite creatures in infinite interdetermination, modal bodies mesh and modify their other, modal minds striving to interpret corporeal encounter. Here, we may correctly speak of matter as the medium of the meaning of things. Mind knows body, and this body is known only through its determinations. The body as object of the mind is the world of perception because in act it is transparency. The seeing eye sees not itself in act but the visible world.[18] The perceived body is a patchwork of the particular senses, the perceiving body, the essential individual as physical agency. In knowing body, mind knows the world.

This dynamic of impingement and self-affirmation, determination and interpretation, that we have been describing, Spinoza identifies, in book III, with his notion of *conatus*.

> The effort by which each thing endeavours to persevere in its own being is nothing but the actual essence of the thing itself.   (prop. 7, III)

> Conatus, quo unaquaeque res in suo esse perseverare conatur, nihil est
> praeter ipsius rei actualem essentiam.   (II, 146, 20)

This effort or appetite for being, which is the essence of each thing, must
be understood as principle of unity.

> Each thing, in so far as it is in itself, endeavours to persevere in its being.
>   (prop. 6, III)

> Unaquaeque res, quantum in se est, in suo esse perseverare contatur.
>   (II, 146, 7)

The power of essence is power as it is *in se*, an intrinsic effort for the
specific quality of being that defines a single, singular individual (schol.
prop. 9 & schol. prop. 57, III). That which is absolutely *in se*, substance
itself, enacts eternity. The inseity of the finite, however, yields neither
eternity nor finite duration. The finite is not *causa sui*, to which alone
pertains the necessary existence of eternity. Finite essence does not
involve existence, and the inseity of the finite cannot be eternal. Yet, as
limited expression of divine immanence, the inseity of even finite essence
cannot involve internal limit. Essence is without self-contradiction. The
life of the finite does not bear within it the measure of its days. Essence
under privation, *conatus* involves indefinite duration.

> The effort by which each thing endeavours to persevere in its own being
> does not involve finite but indefinite time.   (prop. 8, III)

> Conatus, quo unaquaeque res in suo esse perseverare conatur, nullum
> tempus finitum, sed indefinitum involvit.   (II, 147, 2)

No thing contradicts itself. Death does not follow from the source of
being (dem. prop. 8, III). Essence always affirms. The non-being of any
thing is not that thing, but its other (prop. 4, III). For Spinoza, death is
not the limit of finite being, only transcendence is the limit. Duration as
a quantity of existence is not the measure of a thing's reality (schol. prop.
45, II). Duration as a quantity of existence is abstracted from the
qualitative duration of the living thing. It is this qualitative duration that
is essence as appetite. Durational existence is desire. This is the meaning
of *conatus*.

Spinoza does not deny the reality of duration. The movements out of
which we abstract measure and time are the real activity of actual
individuals, struggling for cohesion in the interplay of joys and sorrows.
Indeed, pleasure and pain are, finally, the proof of the reality of
duration.

Yet, unlike the perfect and eternal being of the whole, duration, the being of the part, must be paradox. Eternity is the being of the one. Duration is the being of a one among many. This quality of existence demands the other. Spinoza writes:

> The human mind does not know the human body itself, nor does it know that the body exists, except through ideas of affections by which the body is affected.   (prop. 19, II)

> Mens humana ipsum humanum Corpus non cognoscit, nec ipsum existere scit, nisi per ideas affectionum, quibus Corpus afficitur.   (II, 107, 30)

The perception of durational existence derives from perception of external objects. The encountered other remains present until eclipsed by some further other (prop. 17, II). Thus, the present presence of another generates the perception of phenomenal existence. One exists, i.e., knows durational existence, only in so far as one experiences the presence of others. The present is the presence of the other. Durational existence generates out of infinite interrelations.

In the plurality of sense, the partiality of self and the power of the other, we see adumbrated the absolutely achieved multiplicity of the divine nature. God manifests in infinite attributes under infinite modification. This plenitude expresses directly the transcendent unity of substance, a unity reflected in the idea of God, God's consciousness of Himself as all in one. The finite being, as being in God, has not the infinite inseity of *causa sui*, and cannot know in absolute unity. For man, desire, the consciousness of *conatus*, is the unificatory power whereby finite self achieves its limit as limited whole. Mind strives to know body, to know mind knowing body, strives for access to certainty of being, to be certain of the world. Spinoza's doctrine of epistemic transcendence is a doctrine of the true body, for the essence of the body is the world of conception. The essence of the body is the meaning of the body's presence in the phenomenal realm.

CHAPTER SEVEN

KINDS OF KNOWLEDGE

Before we may consider Spinoza's picture of affective life, the dynamic of moral struggle and release, we must examine the doctrine of epistemic transcendence, the bases of which have been set forth in the preceding discussion of one and other.

The individual is a one, body and mind aspects of a single being (schol. prop. 7; prop. 11; & corol. prop. 13, II). Yet, it is a one among many, its conative unity a power of reagency. We have already suggested that the necessarily incomplete knowledge that the part has of whole involves an othering of self, the alienation of a being from its intrinsic inseity. Spinoza's account of the three kinds of knowledge integrates the spectrum of experience into a principle of self-unification and transcendence of partiality.

In the second scholium to proposition 40, part II, Spinoza sets forth a schema of the functioning of human *conatus* as thought, man's intelligence of the world. The categories of knowledge, Spinoza introduces in terms of the unification of a many into a one. He writes, 'We perceive many things and form universal ideas . . .' (schol. 2 prop. 40, II).

Knowledge of the first kind, imagination or opinion, involves the formation of universal ideas from sensed particulars and from signs. Man's mental *conatus* is the constant struggle of consciousness to conceive its experience, to understand that which it experiences rather than to be overcome by it. In the first kind of knowledge, we observe the tendency of our attempt to control our experience by including in a general class individuals that we have not understood. Opinion is the unification of imagined similarity. As the egocentric reading of one individual in the common order of nature, it does not articulate authentic sameness. This becomes possible only in the second kind of knowledge, reason, which is based in common notions, in insight into ontologically valid sameness.

In the common order of nature, knowledge reflects the immediate determination of a particular body (corol. 2, prop. 16, II), encoded by a pattern of association (prop. 18 with schol., II). It is the fragmented perception of a self alienated from the intrinsic order of the intellect. Extrinsically conditioned, the thoughts of the imaginal self are caused by others it encounters and by the others it is: it remains determined by impingement and the disruptions implicit in its composition out of other simpler selves. Its ideas are inadequate (prop. 34, II). Its knowledge is false (props. 35 & 41, II).

The order of intellect is an order of intrinsic causation (prop. 1, III), which penetrates the essential concatenation of causes (schol. prop. 18, II). In so far as man transcends the forces of temporally conditioned desire, he becomes wholly himself, adequate cause of his ideas, and the ideas, absolute in him, are wholly adequate and true (prop. 34, II). This is the inseity of human cognitive activity that paraphrases the divine inseity of absolute adequation and total truth, expressing the meaning of human mind as part participating in the intellect of God (corol. prop. 11, II). All ideas are true in God (prop. 32, II). All ideas in God in so far as He constitutes the essence of the human mind are in us true (dem. prop. 34, II).

Man's power to understand truly is, then, the unimpeded agency of human essence as expression of the divine nature. To follow the order of intellect is to achieve ontic self-definition as mode of God. True knowledge is realized immanence.

Yet, the very world that overcomes the individual, for the privation of knowledge is only the profusion of being, is, for the finite creature, the necessary ground of any knowing. We have seen that, for Spinoza, the world is embodied as the body of the individual. The body as partial reflection of the infinite community of nature derives actuality from its others, and is itself constituted by the shared properties that define it within the continuum of substance. These are the common properties of which Spinoza writes, the bases of reason.

> Those things which are common to everything, and which are equally in the part and in the whole, can only be adequately conceived.   (prop. 38, II)

> Illa, quae omnibus communia, quaeque aeque in parte, ac in toto sunt, non possunt concipi, nisi adaequate.   (II, 118, 20)

From lemma 2, II, and its demonstration, we learn that all bodies agree in that they involve the conception of extension and are related to motion and rest. From the community of bodies, the kinetic laws of their interaction, we derive principles for valid unifications of the 'many things' perceived. The rational science of space interprets God as extension, articulating the unity of nature as system of causal derivation. Likewise, a science of mind, based upon the common properties of consciousness, explicates the unity of nature as determinate causal order of thought. From the necessarily adequate ideas of common properties follow other necessarily adequate ideas (prop. 40, II), yielding those special sciences concerned with the properties of various types of things (schol. prop. 40, II)

Here, it must be emphasized that these common properties are not only the basis of adequate idea, but of the possibility of any experience whatsoever. Without shared properties of being, no individual exists. Further, it is as causal agency that these properties generate existence. Man's active possession of certain common notions, his necessary conception of authentic aspects of being (prop. 39, II), is his reality as man, as an organism of a particular grade of complexity. Man's mind in so far as it is his, is a concept. It is idea as action (expl. def. 3, II). This concept is his reality as thought, as the vigilant unity of his body is his reality as extension.[19]

The first and second kind of knowledge, then, involve the unification of multiplicity by the use of universals. The imaginal universals, unlike the rational, falsify in their unification. They are not justified by the causal community of substance. Nevertheless, even the rational universals remain abstract and hypothetical. They are ideas about unity, not insight into unity itself. Spinoza identifies unity always with the concrete being of the individual. Indeed, these three terms may be deemed interchangeable in discourse on Spinoza. Where we have unity, we have an individual, and only the individual is concrete, only the individual is an *ens reale*.

Thus, the third kind of knowledge has no recourse to universals. It is direct intuition into the essences of individual things.

> This kind of knowing advances from an adequate idea of the formal essence of certain attributes of God to the adequate knowledge of the essence of things.   (schol. 2 prop. 40, II)

> Atque hoc cognoscendi genus procedit ab adaequata idea essentiae formalis quorundam Dei attributorum ad adaequatam cognitionem essentiae rerum.
> (II, 122, 16)

In the fifth book of the *Ethic*, we learn that this intuition of individual objects is also the ultimate realization of the essence of God, the absolute unification of the mind with nature that is love. The intellectual love of God is proof of Him in a sense that the valid but abstract proofs of reason cannot be (schol. prop. 36, V).

According to Spinoza, the human mind possesses an adequate knowledge of the eternal and infinite essence of God as the absolute common property of all existents (dem. prop. 46, II). All rational thought has reference to God. Reason, through the exploration of logical entailment, the articulation and interrelation of common notions, synthesizes a body of adequate idea, a logical system reflecting the structure of the whole. This logical activity has ontological status, representing an access in power. At a point of power, of understanding, reason blossoms into intuitive science.

In intuitive science, insight into the essence of things becomes knowledge of God as participation in the concrete reality of divine being. All rational thought expresses an inseity of knowing mind, and, in intuitive science, the knowledge of God involves perfect self-consciousness.

Spinoza's analysis of consciousness and self-consciousness has special import for his doctrine of the three kinds of knowledge. The doctrine of *idea ideae* introduced in proposition 21, II, is, as the scholium suggests, tied to the meaning of certainty as self-confirmation. The doctrine of the idea of the idea is central to Spinoza's explication of the nature of thought.

We have earlier identified the unificatory urge of thought as the dynamic of conative agency. Man seeks to preserve his being by unifying the multiplicity of his experience. The desire to understand is the struggle for the unity of self. For Spinoza, the mind of an individual is not something over and above the ideas that compose it. The mind is this multiplex idea (prop. 15, II). To the finite individual, absolute unity of consciousness is not given, rather, that unity is perpetual conquest of fragmentation. As we have seen, man may attempt this through falsifying imaginal abstraction or, truly, according to the order of intellect. Yet, attempt he must, for this attempt is his very being as durational activity. More, this attempt is the finite expression of the true nature of the attribute thought. As man is in and is conceived through God, so the mind of man is continuous with the nature of thought itself. Divine attribute, thought is the eternity of God as perfectly free activity, an infinite unity of being in absolute self-knowledge (dem. prop. 35, V). In man, as in all things, thought works to achieve itself.

All nature is animate. Yet, each mind possesses its specific degree of potency, expresses, according to its complexity, the character of the attribute from which it follows. Self-consciousness cannot, then, be something radically other than the consciousness that even the simplest thing has of itself, rather, consciousness is a continuum of complexity. To understand Spinoza here, we should not try to imagine the mind of a rock or an amoeba. This would be profitless enterprise (section 26, appendix, IV).[20] All it requires is an examination of the range of consciousness we each experience. At times, we achieve insight into the value of the things we encounter. At others, we are submerged, our consciousness dulled and fragmented. The confused awareness of our mental states is neither something wholly other, nor identical with genuine self-consciousness, the individual's power to differentiate itself from its complement in nature.

An individual's consciousness is its awareness of itself as distinct from yet continuous with its environment. The more complex the individual, the more it has in common with everything else (corol. prop. 39, II). This means that the more complex the form of mental energy a mind represents, the greater its capacity to use itself as an instrument of consciousness. In this sense, we may judge the rock's or the amoeba's power of growth far less than man's. Adequate idea generates adequate idea (prop. 40, pt. II), and in man we find a greater power of consciousness to reproduce itself.

The propositions employed by Spinoza in his proof of the *idea ideae*, he has claimed do not 'refer more to man than to other individuals' (schol. prop. 13, II). Proposition 21, II, however, focuses upon the particular self-consciousness of the human mind as a higher power of enjoyment, a power that achieves its limit in the self-confirmation of consciousness. The doctrine of *idea ideae* points ahead to its full explication in proposition 43, II.

> He who has a true idea knows at the same time that he has a true idea, nor can he doubt the truth of the thing.   (prop. 43, II)

> Qui veram habet ideam, simul scit se veram habere ideam, nec rei veritate potest dubitare.   (II, 123, 17)

Beyond imagination, the human mind takes hold of itself. As fulfillment of the nature of consciousness itself, certainty is the highest expression of individuality.

We note that genuine self-consciousness involves the conception of a true idea (schol. prop. 21, II). Consciousness, for Spinoza, is not self-reflexive as an abstract subjectivity.[21] Consciousness is defined as consciousness of an object. The idea of the idea, as mind's awareness of itself, is the individual's power to distance itself from its immediate experience, to grasp the value of things apart from their immediate impact. The interaction with an object becomes true knowledge of it. The idea of the idea is not, however, necessarily this attained awareness itself. We may describe it as the structural 'possibility' of awareness. The *idea ideae* is not necessarily adequate.[22]

Spinoza proves that:

> The order and connection of ideas is the same as the order and connection of things.   (prop. 7, II)

> Ordo, & connexio idearum idem est, ac ordo, & connexio rerum.   (II, 89, 21)

To have an idea of an object is to interact with it. Yet, the ideas had by finite man cannot all be true ideas. This privation of knowledge is not overcome by the mind's union with itself in *idea ideae*, but can be carried into the sphere of self-awareness. Self-consciousness is not self-knowledge.

Man's inseity is knowledge according to the order of intellect, his unity or essence identical with the essence of reason, the mind itself in so far as it clearly and distinctly understands (dem. prop. 26, IV). In so far as man has adequate ideas, he necessarily acts (prop. 1, III). Adequate cause of his own knowledge, he freely realizes the essence of human virtue. He creates himself. The power of the mind is, then, really that mind's creativity, not creativity as a kind of indeterminate freedom, but as determinate activity, the mind as act of self-generation. Certainty, knowledge intrinsically substantiated, is the true creativity of consciousness, the individual's attainment of its limit in active essence.

CHAPTER EIGHT

FREEDOM AS ONTIC LIMIT

Spinoza's rejection of freedom of the will follows from the causal determinism in which he posits the unity of nature (prop. 32, I & prop. 48, II). Nothing in nature is free with this kind of arbitrary discontinuity. Everything in nature is defined by its necessary continuity with the whole. Thus is every volition a determinate mode of substance.

Further, this causal determinism must be understood in terms of the intrinsic dynamic of essence. Essence, divine or human, is causal activity. Causation is being as the generation of being.

Nothing exists from whose nature an effect does not follow.   (prop. 36, I)

Nihil existit, ex cujus natura aliquis effectus non sequatur.   (II, 77, 13)

While only God exists as *causa sui*, essential cause of His own existence, and the existence of finite things does not follow from their essence, we must see how Spinoza conceives the existence of each individual as a function of its essential identity. Finite existence is infinitely conditioned, but all being, in the part as in the whole, must, in a certain sense, be infinite. There is no finite being. Even the finite must be an expression of essence as infinite potency to generate existence (prop. 4, III). The continuity of anything with itself, its power to sustain identity durationally, is this very causality. The finite endures as conditioned infinite (prop. 8, III). From this, it follows that all experience, if only partially, is an expression of a thing's power of existence. When Spinoza speaks of suffering, we must note that, though suffering and act are contrasted, radical suffering is a contradiction in terms. A thing is always determined in so far as it acts. The durational existence of the mode is its creativity as partial expression of the eternal constitutive creativity of God.

Here, we must turn to Spinoza's account of human experience and knowledge, emotion and understanding, his continuous psychology-epistemology, to consider the causal explication of passivity and activity in the context of which we develop this interpretation of God's immanence. We must turn to the phenomenal, that is, to the operations of imagination in the constitution of the objects of emotion, in order to understand transcendence by knowledge of the mind's true object.

Experience, as axiom 3, part II, already shows, is intentional. Consciousness always involves an object, and at the basis of all emotion is thought itself. Thus, emotion involves an object, an idea of what is loved, hated, desired. The infinite dynamic of affect as determination reflects the infinity of things following from God's nature. Proposition 56, III, reads:

> Of joy, sorrow, and desire, and consequently of every effort which either, like vacillation of mind, is compounded of these, or, like love, hatred, hope, and fear, is derived from them, there are just as many kinds as there are objects by which we are affected.   (prop. 56, III)

> Laetitiae, Tristitiae, & Cupiditatis, & consequenter uniuscujusque affectus, qui ex his componitur, ut amini fluctuationis, vel qui ab his derivatur, nempe Amoris, Odii, Spei, Metus, &c. tot species dantur, quot sunt species objectorum, a quibus afficimur.   (II, 184, 16)

The constitution of the object of emotion is to be understood in terms of causality. At the beginning of the *Ethic*'s third part Spinoza sets forth his definitions of adequate and inadequate cause and of affect as act or passion. The effect of an adequate cause can be clearly and distinctly conceived by means of that cause. The effect of an inadequate cause cannot be so conceived. When an individual is the adequate cause of anything done within or without, it acts, when inadequate cause, it suffers. The acts and passions of the individual, its affects, are the modifications of the body which increase or decrease, help or hinder, its power of acting, together with the ideas of these modifications. Here, we observe that the epistemological analogue and expression of adequate cause is adequate idea, of inadequate cause, mutilated and confused idea (expl. gen. def. of affects, III). Spinoza presents a complex and rigorously consistent reading of the causal import of all levels of knowledge.

Each human mind has its specific body as ideate and perceives alone its modifications (prop. 19, II), that is, the mind perceives its specific body as modified, as determined by, other bodies (corols. 1 & 2 prop. 16, II). A part of the infinite causal network of the whole, the human mind can know adequately neither the body itself nor the determining bodies in themselves (props. 19 & 23–27, II). So also, at this level, neither can mind know itself (props. 28 & 29, II). Spinoza shows here both how knowledge begins in sense perception and why at this level the mind can grasp neither the form of the body nor its own form. In imagination, the infinite creativity of God, His infinite power of differentiation, expresses itself in the finite individual's inability to penetrate the true order of causality.

The association of ideas defines the dynamic of the affective life (prop.

18, II; props. 14–17, III). The individual endures, experiencing si-
multaneity as ordering principle of consciousness, experiences a determined linkage of presences. The power of others marks the self, and the
traces of these others determine us to experience them as present until
eclipsed by some stronger affect (prop. 17, II; prop 18, III; props. 5–7,
IV). Experience has momentum.

The individual struggles to assimilate the impact of things and of
ideas, seeking to persevere in existence (prop. 6, III). This effort to
persevere in its own being is the very essence of the thing itself (prop. 7,
III). It is its 'appetite' for being, for its own specific being (schol. prop. 9,
III). Each desires reality and experiences the mind's passage to greater
and lesser degrees of being, of power, as joy and sorrow (affects, defs. 2 &
3, III). The human person as complex individual can be affected by joy
or sorrow as a whole or can experience the affection of some part, its joy
or sorrow, as titillation or pain (schol. prop. 11, III).

These, joy, sorrow, and desire, Spinoza designates the primary affects
from which all others derive (schol. prop. 11, III). From the nature of the
individual as desire, it follows that every organism endeavors to enjoy joy
and avoid sorrow (props. 11–13 & 28, III). It seeks to imagine those
things which enhance or increase its power of acting and to exclude those
which hinder or diminish it.

For the human person, the struggle of consciousness to do so must be
seen in terms of the mind's struggle to understand. Mind is activity;
thus, the idea constituting the human mind is the continual attempt to
fully conceive experience (expl. def. 3, II). At the level of imagination,
the level at which mind is to the greatest degree conditioned by others
rather than self-determining, this cannot be attained. Association of
ideas rules. Yet, for the complex human consciousness, association takes
the form of interpretation.

The human mind as highly differentiated form of idea is conscious of
its *conatus* in a manner in which simpler organisms are not (prop. 9, III &
prop. 8, IV). What in the less complex must be a primitive concatenation
of images, is for man, interpretation. We may even say that culture,
certainly in part, represents such an associative pattern. We react in
ontologically determined ways, but it is within a cultural context that we
have our ideas of pleasure and injury, of right and wrong. Here, Spinoza
speaks of the import of custom in affective life. He writes:

> Custom and religion are not the same everywhere; but, on the contrary,
> things which are sacred to some are profane to others, and what are
> honourable with some are disgraceful with others. Education alone, there-
> fore, will determine whether a man will repent of any deed or boast of it.
> (affects, expl. def. 27, III)

Nam consuetudo, & Religio non est omnibus eadem; sed contra, quae apud alios sacra, apud alios profana, & quae alios honesta, apud alios turpia sunt. Prout igitur unusquisque educatus est, ita facti alicujus poenitet, vel eodem gloriatur.   (II, 197, 20)

Our response to the object involves an interpretation. We must take the object in a certain way. These interpretations, however, do not arise from any free decree of the mind (prop. 48, II). They are themselves determinate elements of response. Interpretations are determined, each representing a particular locus in an infinite psychological complex. Spinoza gives an ontological account and valuation of culture and interpretation as forms of imagination.

We imagine a person is this. We love, we hate, we desire, the imaginary other. It is the other we experience, the impact of his energy, and though the idea of Peter in Paul is not a direct manifestation of the essence of Peter but of the essence of Paul (schol. prop. 17, II), it is Peter's power that determines Paul in its proportion to Paul's own power; the force of the other in proportion to the force of the self determines the strength of the affect (props. 16 & 17, II; props. 5–7, IV). Yet, at this level, Peter and Paul are images one to the other. They have nothing in common. There is no community of mind. It is most in imagination, this associative pattern of affect at the level of duration, that we encounter other objects, other persons.

The human mind remains, however, always the struggle of conscious-ness to push past imagination, of the power by which the mind imagines to force its way through to the ground of imagining, of psychic energy to achieve itself. To interpret is to say what a thing is. It is to give a causal account.

The body with its affects is the object of the mind. The mind is the idea of the affected body. As mind, the human person assimilates experience by understanding it. The person seeks to assimilate the impact of other parts of nature by explicating causal relations. We here understand the sense in which the modifying object becomes, for the human being, the object of thought, of emotion.

Spinoza writes:

> *Love* is nothing but joy accompanied with the idea of an external cause, & *hatred* is nothing but sorrow with the accompanying idea of an external cause.   (schol. prop. 13, III)

> Nempe *Amor* nihil aliud *est*, quam *Laetitia, concomitante idea causae externae*; & *Odium* nihil aliud, quam *Tristitia, concomitante idea cause externae*. (II, 151, 5)

Thus, the determined ascription of causal agency is especially central to the forms of human emotional experience. Such ascriptions involve the mistaken notions of causality and freedom found at the first level. The individual, unable to grasp the manifold of determination constituting any passion, identifies some limited aspect of his experience as its cause, and the emotion which takes this 'cause' as object is increased or diminished in proportion as he imagines it sole cause (prop. 48, III). Further, to take an individual as sole cause is to perceive it through itself and without others, i.e., to imagine it free (prop. 49, III). This misplaced idea of freedom accounts for the particular intensity of relationships among persons (schol. prop. 49, III).

The complexity of determination involved in association as interpretation appears with special clarity in emotions of self-interpretation, emotions in which the individual is his own object in this further sense. Spinoza's treatment of such emotions as self-contentment and repentance illustrates the role played by an individual's self-ascription, showing the form of experience generated in an individual's understanding himself as cause of others' joy and sorrow. The further definitions of self-exaltation and shame analyze the nature of a man's experience when he ascribes to himself the causal ascriptions made by others of his kind (schol. prop. 30, III). The configuration of reality determines the individual to give a particular reading of causal relation, which as pattern of impingement cannot reflect the true causal order of nature. At the first level of knowledge, experience is fragmentary and does not grasp the underlying unity that makes experience possible. The mind synthesizes false wholes. Only when unified according to the order of the intellect, in power and not in passion, does the mind penetrate and express the true order of causality.

Imagining is presence, the cause, that through which presence is read, for imagination necessarily contemplates its object as actually existing, as present (prop. 17, II), and cause is that through which an object is understood as brought into being, as posited in presence (ax. 4, I; props. 9–13, IV). Thus, the categories of causal explication correspond to the valences of the affective life. Indeed, finally, the form of human freedom from the bondage of affect involves the affective status of causal interpretation. Here, we must emphasize the nature of imagining as a range of creativity. For Spinoza, imagining encompasses a spectrum of experience. The imagining individual suffers more or less, is more or less aware, more or less creative. The human mind as complex idea represents a higher power of creativity than the amoeba, hence the range of human imaginative experience is broader. Even to give a misreading of the causal relationships constituting one's experience expresses a higher level of mental power than that possessed by the amoeba. Imagination concerns the impact of others, which we struggle to assimilate. At times, the external force is too strong, and the human being's power of understanding is radically minimized. At other times, his creativity perseveres to the level of a misunderstanding of the causal constituents of his experience.

These causal accounts, which, as we have seen, are themselves determinate, play an important role in the dynamics of emotion. Necessity, possibility and contingency are, in effect, categories equivalent respectively to affirmation of an object's existence through its essence or cause, incomplete idea of the cause by which an object must be produced, and idea of the object in isolation from any cause (schol. 1 prop. 33, I; defs., 3 & 4, props. 11-13, IV). Our readings of causal status together with our readings of temporal status determine the intensity of our response to any idea (props. 9-13, IV). The first level of experience is a pattern of linkage and eclipse. The pattern of association determining the individual constitutes his sense of time (schol. prop. 44, II; schols. 1 & 2 prop. 18, III), and here temporal and spatial distance play an identical role in determining the intensity of affect (def. 6, props. 9 & 10, IV). Just so, at the level of imagination, causal interpretation reflects the associative principle with presence as the affective maximum.

The passional reading of reality follows from the individual's perspective as a limited part of an infinite whole. The active understanding of reality follows from the individual's fulfillment of its own law as itself a whole. We see that according to Spinoza these cannot, for the finite individual, represent radical opposites. Were the individual not a whole, there could be no experience. Yet, the individual as whole remains also part, and there can be no final transcendence of suffering. Man is a part of nature (props. 2 & 4, IV). For this reason, his struggle for freedom from the bondage of affect must incorporate the energy of the emotional life through his understanding of its laws.

That the individual represents a psychical/physical unity in which the order and connection of ideas is the same as the order and connection of things (prop. 1, V) means that by detaching his affects from the thoughts of external causes and connecting them with other thoughts, the individual can conceive clear and distinct ideas of these affects (props. 2-4, V). He can be adequate cause of his own ideas. In this, he constitutes reality in the form of his own power: he acts. Arranging experience according to the order of the intellect, the individual articulates its being according to the laws of its own nature.

The order of the intellect is an order of necessity (prop. 44. II). At this level, the mind as cause of its own consciousness expresses the form of its specific necessity, recognizing that necessity by which all follows from the divine nature, recognizing God as cause. In so far as the mind does this, it has greater control over the affects (prop. 6, V), and, so long as its capacity to understand is not hindered by contrary affect, can arrange them according to this powerful order of act (prop. 10, V). Finally, the order of act, the structure of human experience, through the connection of the clear and distinct idea of every affect with the idea of God, becomes a persistent meditation upon the divine nature (props. 11–16, V).

Yet, Spinoza is true to the integrity of emotion. Our understanding in so far as it is true can displace no affect (prop. 14, IV). God's truth is everywhere. God is all truth. All experience is the truth of God. Our understanding can only displace affect as itself stronger opposed affect (prop. 7, IV). The truth of the necessity present in the higher forms of knowledge is, however, grounded in the common notions, the common properties of things which can only be experienced by us as present, and presence is the constitutive impulse of imagination (dem. prop. 7 & prop. 8, V). Further, the connection of the idea of God to every affect utilizes the law of association to draw the energies of imagination upward to higher levels (prop. 13, V). Reason transforms affects, and intuitive science transforms reason. For Spinoza, the highest level of knowing transforms all levels, while they yet remain true to their own dynamic. Thus, though man is a part of nature, 'infinitely surpassed by the power of external causes' (prop. 3, IV), because affect as act expresses more being than the pattern of passion, man perseveres in his desire to understand (schol. prop. 10, V).

Man's power may thus be conceived as activity and passivity. We have seen that even suffering is a kind of activity. For in man, as in all things, divine immanence is act. Only in this sense can God be truth without suffering (prop. 17, V). If God is infinite interdetermination, if nature is a whole in which everything affects everything else, each part must have its integrity, each part must be conceived in terms of activity.

The attainment of sufficient complexity and individuation is, for Spinoza, clearly requisite for activity as adequate causation, but, in the parts of *causa sui*, we find partiality and privation, no negation. The modes are God's acts.

The determinate being of divine substance issues in the fully determined being of mode. Spinoza has denied that God acts from freedom of will (corol. 1 prop. 32, I). His unity, infinitude, perfection preclude this. The truth of eternity is an absolute realization of being, for which there can be no this *or* that, no one *or* the other. Eternity is everything.

We have earlier shown the derivation of duration from eternity. The import of this derivation for the meaning of human freedom becomes evident when we contrast the notion of freedom of the will with Spinoza's account of durational being.

Duration is not outside eternity. It is not a falling away from eternal being. Duration cannot be conceived as a field of arbitrary choice. Neither God nor man acts from freedom of will. The possibility of moral action and of epistemic transcendence does not lie in empty space, but in the vital continuity of plenum.

All ideas are true in God, but we have seen that the living mind of man cannot be constituted solely by true ideas. Man experiences his incompleteness in the multilated and confused knowledge of inadequate ideas. He 'knows' falsely.

In the demonstration of proposition 35, part II, Spinoza declares that 'falsity cannot consist in absolute privation.' Absolute privation would mean nothing to think about, and it is the central tenet of Spinoza's theory of mind that mind is always occupied (prop. 17, II). The affirmation of any idea ceases only with its exclusion by another. Durational mind unceasingly imagines presence. There is only eclipse, no empty space. The mind may be said to have a kind of pseudo-space of not-knowing, but this means that it is thinking of something else. Irrational affect blocks the logical traversement of causal concatenation. The mind imagines a reality in violation of the order of being. Intellect must emend itself through realization of the true causal connection of one idea to another.

In the common order of nature, imaginal association is principle of eclipse, but even here ideas are no 'dumb pictures on a tablet' (schol. prop. 49, II). Inadequate ideas involve the active being of the mode. The passivity of the mode is its *non*-being and the being of an other. Association of ideas indicates the passivity of the mode in its encounter with world. It suffers impingement. Yet, all suffering is parasitical upon perseverant *conatus*. Pure passivity would be non-being. The failure of knowledge cannot be divorced from the attempt to know. Of this essential modal activity we have spoken, as also of the nature of thought as nisus to self-confirmation. Transcendence is required of consciousness, and the move to transcendence may itself create the pseudo-space of falsity. Man's mind represents a high level of complexity. To make a mistake is a complex matter.

Falsity does not come from a freely willed affirmation or negation, for there is none 'excepting that which the idea, in so far as it is an idea, involves' (prop. 49, II). Every idea involves active presence.

Only in true ideas, however, is the active presence a realization of the essence of the thinking individual. The individual achieves causal adequacy in the necessary certitude of true ideas. This certitude is not the absence of doubt. We assent to what is false through a blockage of causes for doubt (schol. prop. 49, II). Our idea about a thing remains insufficiently complex. Here, false or true intelligence may cause us to doubt what we think, but certitude is immovable, for it is the intrinsic positivity of truth itself, and, inseparable from the reality of the mind's object, it must express the essential nature of that mind.

This inseity of certainty is the freedom of the mode. The unimpeded agency of the adequate and true idea finds consumation in intuitive science, in certitude most concretely achieved. In the third kind of knowledge, man transcends being as becoming to become the being of himself. He attains the freedom of eternal being in the realization of essence. Freedom is essential being.

We may understand this in terms of limit, limit not as delimitation but as structure. God is the absolute expression of limit. God fulfills His own infinite structure. He is perfect plenum of articulation. We have shown that God's freedom consists in this infinite efficacy of divine essence. Just so, we can speak of the essence of the mode as its limit. Its limit is its level of complexity. Thus, each individual has its specific limit, the eternal form of power by which it endures. This limit is not, then, something above the thing, but its very identity as unique configuration of shared properties of being.

The spectrum of individuals of varying reality and excellence manifests the sense in which there can be greater and lesser infinites. There is not perfect symmetry at the level of the finite modes. Each is characterized by its own singular degree of power. This power is not reducible to its parts. No thing could exist without an infinite power of self-affirmation, and a thing is not infinite, if it is reducible to something else. This failure to explain a thing in terms of its parts is identical with the failure to explain the infinite in terms of number.

That substance is indivisible, the modes infinitely divisible, means there can be differentiation without fracture. The forms of power in the phenomenal world reflect the form of eternity. Even in eternity, some things are more eternal than others. Duration reflects an eternal order of perfection.

Enduring beings, in acts of understanding, we approximate eternal limit. The more the mind understands by the third kind of knowledge, the more it desires to understand by this knowledge, the more it is determined to understand by this knowledge (prop. 26, V). A human mind can become in greater part eternal. One whose mind is so constituted, in so far as he knows his essence to be eternal, cannot fear death (schol. prop. 39, V). He recognizes fortune as the infinite play of God's power and no longer fears change. He is a free man (prop. 67, IV). In knowledge, he has approximated to the infinite limit of the eternal self. Thus, Spinoza writes:

The power of the mind is limited solely by knowledge. (schol. prop. 20, V)

At Mentis potentia sola cognitione definitur.   (II, 293, 25)

In this definition, he contrasts the limit of the thing as delimited by the power of external objects with limit as intrinsic articulation. Here, limit is the enjoyment of a power in a certain sense infinite.

CHAPTER NINE

FLUX AND STRIFE:
THE ETHICAL IMPLICATIONS
OF THE ONE AND THE MANY

The freedom of man is approximation to eternal limit in essence. We have seen that, in this concrete realization of the meaning of man, the human individual attains self-actualization. Spinoza regards this as highest form of *acquiescentia in se ipso* (prop. 52, IV & prop. 27, V). From intuitive science arises the ultimate joy that is no longer the movement to greater perfection (affects, def. 2, III), but the enjoyment of perfection itself (dem. prop. 27, V). It is the point at which duration knows itself eternity. The mode opens out into the continuum of substance to love as the love with which God loves Himself (prop. 36, V).

We find our freedom, our blessedness, in this conscious continuity of love: we rejoice in God's rejoicing in Himself. Spinoza identifies this blessedness with glory in the sacred writings. The equipoise of eternity, God's glory is the perfection of transcendent unity. So likewise, the glory of the human mind is the self-realizing repose of an inseity defined by its active participation in the divine nature (schol. prop. 36, V).

Yet, this is beatitude, not morality. We must turn from eternal order of essence to the experience of existence. The *Ethic* sets forth the truth of man's liberation as the laws of strife. In the world, rationality is a battle for knowledge, for consciousness.

Moral life is not in a vacuum. Indestructible intellectual love is the being of nature, not a part of it (schol. prop. 37, V). It transcends entirely durational existence. The durational existent, however, only expresses under privation the true order of causation. Incomplete and unemended, it is in measure alienated from constitutive community of essence. It knows other as impediment to being. The finite individual lives infinitely at risk.

> There is no individual thing in nature which is not surpassed in strength and power by some other thing, but any individual thing being given, another and stronger is also given, by which the former can be destroyed.
>
> (axiom, IV)

> Nulla res singularis in rerum natura datur, qua potentior, & fortior non detur alia. Sed quacunque data alia potentior, a qua illa data potest destrui.
>
> (II, 210, 25)

The ethical imperative for the finite individual is to strengthen itself. Man must grow into increasingly more potent being through unification of consciousness. His virtue is intrinsic determination according to the order of intellect (prop. 24, IV).

Man's *conatus* toward unification thus founds all virtue (prop. 22, IV), for conative endeavour to perseverance is not other than essence (dem. prop. 22, IV).

> Virtue is human power itself, which is limited by the essence alone of man.
> (dem. prop. 20, IV)

> Virtus est ipsa humana potentia, quae sola hominis essentia definitur.
> (II, 224, 12)

Essence defines virtue.

In his account of body, Spinoza has described essence as a proportion of motion and rest (def., discursus on body, II).

> That which makes the form of an individual is the union of bodies.
> (dem. lem. 4, discursus, II)

> id . . . quod formam Individui constituit, in corporum unione . . . consistit.   (II, 100, 24)

Essence is union, and a thing cannot be reduced to its parts. Essence, as the immutable nature of anything, is its empowering in the plurality of experience, the form of that things's transcendence, for even to endure is to transcend. Essence is the source of unity for the durational being. The finite individual is one as essence, many as existence.

At the level of imagination, and the affective is a necessary dimension of all enworlded individuals, partiality defines the finite. Only *causa sui* is absolute self-sufficiency. Man risks death and requires nourishment, both of body and mind (schol. prop. 18 & appendix, 27, IV). The world composes man's existence. He himself is not other than other. He necessarily encorporates the others he encounters. Only his own power defines in what measure they become him. His power is not infinite of itself, and he cannot know his existence, for it is many other than him.

> The human mind does not involve an adequate knowledge of the parts composing the human body.   (prop. 24, II)

> Mens humana partium, Corpus humanum componentium, adaequatam cognitionem non involvit.   (II, 110, 27)

> The idea of any affection of the human body does not involve an adequate knowledge of the human body itself.   (prop. 27, IV)

> Idea cujuscunque affectionis Corporis humani adaequatam ipsius humani Corporis cognitionem non involvit.   (II, 112, 26)

The ideas of the affections of the human body, in so far as they are related only to the human mind, are not clear and distinct, but confused.
(prop. 28, II)

Ideae affectionum Corporis humani, quatenus ad humanam Mentem tantum referuntur, non sunt clarae, & distinctae, sed confusae. (II, 113, 4)

The idea of the idea of any affection of the human body does not involve an adequate knowledge of the human mind.   (prop. 29, II)

Idea ideae cujuscunque affectionis Corporis humani adaequatam humanae Mentis cognitionem non involvit.   (II, 113, 29)

The impact of Spinoza's doctrine of the finite strikes us. We understand why his account of human essence in terms of the one and the many must be an ethic. We understand the principles and implications of that ethic.

The body, in its multiplicity, is not pure unity. It is a unity of unities, each impelled according to the logic of its own being. The tension of disruption is implicit in the body as it seeks to function as a whole. In our every gesture, the phenomenal composite nature of body becomes evident. We struggle for mastery as the unification of parts, for the control of limbs and muscles that will make a movement ours. So likewise, the mind struggles for psychic integration, struggles to think its own thoughts against the continual demand of the other. Meaning is always pulling outward. We experience as dissolution this tide, this infinite multiplicity pulling us apart, the tide of the many. It is not different now than at death. Every element is riddled with meaning. This is not just my hand, this is not merely my blood. These are systems of meaning purely alien to me. A rich and alien life blossoms as my body. Thus, for each of us, *conatus*, perseverance, is not just a push against impinging others, but the pull to center and retain in equipoise a centrifugally exploding self, its fragments individuals in their own right, moving in infinite other universes of meaning and desire.

Here is the full face of Spinoza's denial of final cause. For Spinoza, the hierarchical reading of reality does not obviate an ontic equity of all being (preface, IV). Each thing is perfect. Each thing is a unique expression of the infinite expressiveness. We may distinguish levels of complexity, but, finally, all comparison is abstraction from the concrete continuum of substance.

No one endeavours to preserve his own being for the sake of another object.
(prop. 25, IV)

Nemo suum esse alterius rei causa conservare conatur.   (II, 226, 24)

No individual will relinquish its joy for another (prop. 6, III & dem.

prop. 60, IV).[23] Its *conatus* is its specific power or virtue, the agency through which it participates in the absolute activity of God. This transcendent dynamism is the exclusion of suffering from the divine nature (prop. 17, V), the immutability of God (corol. 2 prop. 20, I). The rich indifference of nature is the love of God (prop. 19, V).[24]

Every individual is made up of a range of other individuals, each determined to love that which feeds its joy (prop. 28, III). The phenomenal self is not pure unity. It can never be absolutely unified. This is why, though the impingement of sense is the image of the infinite, it must be transcended. We must accept the ambiguity of our existence, for we cannot make the world ours, and must commit ourselves to the hierarchy of values that is the structure of our transcendence. For man, as finite individual, unification of self is hierarchy of value. There are ideas that are ours that we cannot possess: these we must relinquish. We must relinquish that in our experience we cannot understand. Man may recognize the infinite power of God in the wild profusion of thought and sensation, but he must be willing to reject some objects of experience, some aspects of self, as of less value. Man transcends through true knowledge of good and evil (preface, IV).

The divine nature posits an ontological fullness of being at every moment. From this, we necessarily conclude the abstract and relative nature of the knowledge of good and evil. It is based upon comparison, and all comparison abstracts from the true nature of substance (preface, IV). Good and evil are *entia rationis*.

This is why the true knowledge of good and evil cannot restrain affect (prop. 14, IV). Abstract or rational knowledge (schol. prop. 62, IV) cannot be fully objective, with objectivity signifying scientific intuition into essence. Neither good nor evil are things in nature. Hence, they cannot be objects of knowledge. Knowledge of good and evil must lack intrinsic causal efficacy (prop. 36, I).

> No affect can be restrained by the true knowledge of good and evil in so far as it is true, but only in so far as it is considered as an affect. (prop. 14, IV)

> Vera boni, & mali cognitio, quatenus vera, nullum affectum coercere potest, sed tantum, quatenus ut affectus consideratur.   (II, 219, 19)

The falsity of imagination is partiality, not privation: the positive presence contained in the false idea cannot be negated (prop. 1, IV). It is part of God's truth (dem. prop. 1, IV).

Yet, man may liberate himself from the bondage of affect through correct causal interpretation. Separating his affects from the idea of external cause forced upon him by the common order of nature, he comes to understand the true dynamic of affect. The necessities of reason, grounded in the common properties of things, become a powerful and constant influence upon his emotions, the more so as all experience must express these common properties and, in them, the universal immanence of God. With increasing potency for unification, man orders feeling in terms of true understanding of his causal identity. Thus, he passes into intuitive knowledge of his dependence upon the divine nature to partake of an immutable and eternal love (schol. prop. 20, V).

This apex of man's freedom cannot, we know, be referred to good and evil. Where there are only adequate ideas, there can be no conception of evil (corol. prop. 64, IV), and, hence, no conception of good (dem. prop. 68, IV). The field of moral struggle and growth is the world of infinite causal interdetermination.

> It is impossible that a man should not be a part of nature, and that he should suffer no changes but those which can be understood through his own nature alone, and of which he is the adequate cause.   (prop. 4, IV)
>
> Fieri non potest, ut homo non fit Naturae pars, & ut nullas possit pati mutationes, nisi, quae per solam suam naturam possint intelligi, quarum-que adaequata sit causa.   (II, 212, 28)

Only in the realm of becoming, is there joy and sorrow, is there becoming better and becoming worse. It is to facilitate preference for the good, that which truly empowers us as men, that we desire to form 'an idea of man upon which we man look as a model of human nature' (preface, IV).

At this juncture, we must take up the central question of our study, the problem of human essence, the 'form of man.' We turn to ask the relation of ideal man, as *ens rationis*, to the essential nature of man, exploring the relevance of Spinoza's account of individuals and universals to the immortality of the mind.

CHAPTER TEN

THAT WHICH IS COMMON

The much debated question of Spinoza's status as either nominalist or realist cannot be settled by identifying him as one or other in accord with some predefined conception of nominalism and realism.[25] The tremendous complexity of Spinoza's account of individuals and universals demands detailed exegesis. Further, Spinoza's preparedness to publish the *Ethic* does not indicate that it is an exhaustively complete work.[26] We shall find, together with claims we may make with certainty, questions that cannot be resolved within the circle of the *Ethic*, or, indeed, through its study in light of Spinoza's other writings.

We state with certainty that, for Spinoza, only individuals are real. We must ask, however, what does Spinoza mean by individual?

As *Ethic*, I, propositions 21 through 23 prove, by individual he does not mean merely finite individuals. The mediate and immediate infinite modes are infinite individuals. The attributes themselves, as expressing the essence of the absolute individual, must be understood as most concretely individual individual. Irreducible to one another, God's attributes express, each uniquely, one unique individual. Indeed, their irreducibility, one to the other, derives from their identity. Each attribute is the essence of substance, therefore, through each attribute that essence may be perceived (def. 4, I).

Spinoza, then, explicitly sets before us a hierarchy of infinite individuality. The attribute thought generates infinite intellect, which generates the idea of God (prop. 1, II; prop. 30, I; prop. 31, I; prop. 4, II). The attribute extension generates motion and rest, which generates the eternal dynamic complex of moving things, the *facies totius universi* (prop. 2, II; corol. 2 prop. 32, I; axiom 1 following prop. 13 & schol. lem. 7, discurus on body, II).

As we have learned from Spinoza's rejection of final cause, God is being most concrete, and the modes most directly derived from Him, concrete in order of their dependence. Like God, the infinite modes are eternal, immutable individuals (props. 21-23, I). It is, thus, as concrete universal singulars that these modes are common throughout nature.[27] Further, as the entire body of the *Ethic* makes clear, they have causal status in the generation of mutable, finite things. Through the infinite modes, all things come to be, and, through them, the essence of each and every thing must be conceived. They are the bases of all rational definition, for they are the common properties of things, which we have seen correspond to the common notions of reason.

Here, we must consider in some detail the relation between this modal hierarchy of universal singulars and the common notions. Can the common notions be identified with these modes or is their relation more complex?

First, however, we must clarify Spinoza's intent in proposition 37 of part II.

> That which is common to everything . . . , and which is equally in the part and in the whole, forms the essence of no individual thing. (prop. 37, II)

> Id, quod omnibus commune . . . , quodque aeque in parte, ac in toto est, nullius rei singularis essentiam constituit.   (II, 118, 10)

This proposition appears to suggest that the common notions must be abstract universals, i.e., that they cannot express infinite singulars as we have argued. Application of the second definition of part II obviates this conclusion. This definition posits the reciprocity of essence and existence as the rule of their distinction.

> I say that to the essence of anything pertains that, which being given, the thing itself is necessarily posited, and being taken away, the thing is necessarily taken; or, in other words, that, without which the thing can neither be nor be conceived, and which in its turn cannot be nor be conceived without the thing.   (def. 2, II)

> Ad essentiam alicujus rei id pertinere dico, quo dato res necessario ponitur, & quo sublato res necessario tollitur; vel id, sine quo res, et vice versa quod sine re, nec esse nec concipi potest.   (II, 84, 17)

With his 'vice versa' Spinoza affirms both the difference between essence and existence and their necessary interrelation. *Quid sit?* and *An sit?* must be distinguished, but they cannot be divorced. For no existent, is existence abstract. It is ever an expression of its identity. The reciprocity of essence and existence holds for the infinite and for the finite, the enduring and the eternal. Only in the case of God, however, does this reciprocity involve necessary existence. In the case of the modes, reciprocity involves, rather, the absolute dependence of their essence and existence on God (prop. 25, I). The existence of a finite thing does not follow from its essence. As our discussion of *conatus* has shown, this does not mean its essence and existence are fractured one from the other. The perseverance of the mode is its essence, essence under privation as the experience of the phenomenal, of duration. It means that a different causal account must be given of the essence and the existence of the finite

thing (prop. 8, II; prop. 28 & schol. 2 prop. 8, I). Spinoza is telling us
that a finite thing cannot be conceived without God, but also that it
cannot be derived *a priori* from His idea.[28]

The demonstration of proposition 37, II, shows Spinoza's claim that
the common forms the essence of no individual thing equivalent to his
claim that a finite thing cannot be derived *a priori* from God. In other
words, the essence and existence of the common does not depend upon
any finite thing.[29] The concrete universality of any infinite mode cannot
be limited by the meaning or duration of a finite individual. No
particular exhausts infinite individuality.

That the common depends upon or expresses an infinite singular does
not, however, necessitate the identification of these singulars with the
common properties, in any event, not an absolute identification of one
infinite mode to one common property. Such an absolute identification
would necessitate positing infinite modes not explicitly presented in the
Ethic.

Our discussion of the three kinds of knowledge has given us a general
understanding of the place of common notions/properties in Spinoza's
theory of knowledge and metaphysics as a whole. This account of the role
of common notion in Spinoza's epistemology and metaphysics will not,
however, suffice. We must be able to say whether a given concept is a
common notion and to generate additional common notions. Without
this ability, we cannot be said to understand what Spinoza is talking
about.

The statement of common properties of bodies in the demonstration of
lemma 2 of the discursus on body in the second part of the *Ethic* is
Spinoza's most explicit indication of what he accounts a common notion.

> All bodies agree in this, that they involve the conception of one and the
> same attribute . . . . They have, moreover, this in common, that they are
> capable generally of motion and rest, and of motion at one time quicker and
> at another slower.   (dem. lem. 2, discurus, II)

> In his enim omnia corpora conveniunt, quod unius, ejusdemque attributi
> conceptum involvant. . . . Deinde, quod jam tardius, jam celerius, &
> absolute jam moveri, jam quiescere possunt.   (II, 98, 4)

Propositions 37 through 39, II, demonstrate that the ideas of these
properties are common notions. Thus, extension, motion, rest are
identified as common notions. Simple ideas, these common notions are
primitive first concepts of the intellect.[30]

Spinoza employs the term common notion in an additional sense. He
calls the laws of logical necessity common notions.[31] It is clear, however,
that for Spinoza these logical laws are propositional expressions of the

essence of the individual. The statement, 'God or substance necessarily exists' does not have a different meaning than 'God' or 'substance' properly understood. Thus, by this use of common notion, we are referred again to the ordering of nature through community of essence that we are trying to understand. Common notion as universal axiom leads back to the properties of actual things.

Two interlocking questions here demand response. First, what is the relation of the common notions to the attributes and the infinite modes? Second, are the common notions concepts of absolute community or do they express a hierarchical ordering of nature?

Spinoza speaks not only of what is common to all bodies, but also of what is common 'to the human body and certain external bodies,' demonstrating that ideas of properties common to the human body and to the external bodies by which it is generally affected are adequate (prop. 39, II). From this it follows that the more a body has in common with other bodies, the more will its mind be adapted to perceive (corol. Prop. 39, II).

In this power 'to do or suffer many things' lies the superiority of the complex organism (schol. prop. 13, II). Finally, in the second axiom following the third lemma of the discursus on body, Spinoza refers to the *corpora simplicissima*, distinguished only by motion and rest, i.e., defined by their participation only in the common property motion and rest. This certainly suggests a hierarchy of common properties with qualities of being not present in the simplest bodies generated at increased levels of complexity.

Here, however, we encounter a stricture. It presents itself in the dictum: difference is not in a thing. Infinite divisibility characterizes *natura naturata*. If what is common is equally in the whole and in the part, how can there be any part in which it is not present?

This conflict may be only apparent. The truth of man is realized through the meaning of nature as a whole. Substance is cause par excellence. The whole is the cause, not the sum of its parts. Man does not exhaust the meaning of nature as cell does not exhaust the meaning of man. Yet, that man is not other than nature, and cell not other than man, that part is continuous with whole, makes possible ranges of quality not fully realized at all levels of partiality. The amoeba, the mote of dust, are not fractured from the divine nature. There is not part so simple that in it what is common is not. This simultaneous omnipresence and hierarchical realization of the common reflects the continuity of the divine nature. For Spinoza, what is common must be indivisibly so.

Attribute and infinite mode are indivisibly present throughout nature, for each thing necessarily involves the eternal and infinite essence of God (prop. 45, II), nor is it possible that any limitation render the infinite mode not omnipresent (prop. 21, I). Spinoza calls common properties explicitly only extension, and motion and rest, and this is, indeed, an attribute with its infinite immediate mode. Is Spinoza identifying common properties with a hierarchy of enveloping infinite modes, a hierarchy in which the human mind takes its place as an eternal mode (schol. prop. 40, V)?[32]

In our study of the types of knowledge, we have understood the common notions as active conception of some genuinely shared property. They are the agency of consciousness in active possession of some authentic facet of the real. Can they be directly identified with the infinite modes?

We conclude that they cannot. Certainly, it is these modes that, through common notions, are known, and it is these modes that are the 'proximate causes' of all things, but the common notions themselves are abstract characterizations of that modal nature, not each itself a mode.

Throughout the *Ethic*, Spinoza has spoken of universals expressing that which individual things have in common. For example, in the scholium to proposition 49, II, he writes:

> We have shown that will is a Universal, or the idea by which we explain all individual volitions, that is to say, that which is common to them all.
> (schol. prop. 49, II)

> Ostendimus enim voluntatem ens esse universale, sive ideam, qua omnes singulares volitiones, hoc est, id, quod iis omnibus commune est, explica-
> mus.   (II, 134, 3)

It is a common or universal idea, as is that of intellect, with which will is ultimately identified (schol. prop. 48 & dem. prop. 49, II). We judge that Spinoza holds these rational universals and not the false universals of imagination. False universals express a locus in the common order of nature, a locus of impingement and impotence, the particular mind in egocentric interpretation of temporal existence. Rational universals denote a genuinely shared property and make a grounded ontic claim. The *Ethic* itself posits the status of rational universals, for if all universals were false, the *Ethic* would be void of sense. The *Ethic* is primarily a work of reason, informed and structured by intuitive science, yet universal and abstract in the manner we have been considering.

In his introductory remarks to part III, Spinoza proposes to treat human actions and appetites as if treating lines, planes, and bodies. Human behavior, in its physical and psychical aspects, becomes field intelligible in terms of causal principles, by ontic community described through rational abstraction. Action and appetite can be termed common properties, as can line, plane, body.

As to whether only simple ideas are common notions, we conclude that common notions need not be absolutely primitive terms. There are common notions not immediately evident to all men (schol. 2 prop. 8, I). The common notion as logical law, which we earlier referred to individual essence, expresses the common properties of things in the abstract necessity of the 'interactions' of rational universals. These are the common notions as universal axioms of a rational science.[33] We may take it that common notions represent a collection of inferences from conscious experience. Our experience of body and of mind grounds in a community of essence made explicit in common notions.

If line, plane, body indicate shared properties, then common notions of one type are geometrical terms out of which a spacial account of the individual can be generated. Straight, circle, triangle are not infinite modes, but abstractions from the geometrical meaning of space. They are true but hypothetical, i.e., not grounded in intuition of essence, insights into the nature of the attribute extension.

This interpretation of common notion means that, for Spinoza, in common notions, man grasps the elements whose synthesis depicts ever more fully a given attribute. Quantity, line, plane, figure are the bases of an account of being as geometrical dynamism, as the attribute extension modified by infinite motion and rest. A full understanding of common notion must include the transition from reason to intuitive science. Spinoza's definition of the third kind of knowledge as advancing 'from an adequate idea of the formal essence of certain attributes of God' (schol. 2 prop. 40, II) indicates that this interpretation of common notion gives a coherent explanation of the movement from reason to intuitive science.

Reason achieves the synthesis of common notions as insight into the essence of substance. Thus, as systematic interrelation of the common properties of body, reason attains realization of extension expressed in motion and rest, and as systematic interrelation of the common properties of mind, reason attains realization of thought expressed in infinite intellect. Idea and ideate are certainly, for Spinoza, mental common notion. Further common notions, such as action and appetite, pertain to mind and body together. Indeed, the epistemic union of mind and body yields common notions that can and must be interpreted both as body and as mind, for example, the affects defined in part III, together with the laws of their dynamic. *Conatus* would be such a common notion. Indeed, it is the prime notion from which the affects are deduced. Though the actual *conatus* of each being is the unique essence of that thing (prop. 7, III), we can have a true universal idea of *conatus* as the perseverence of mode. This is an abstract knowledge of the meaning of essence, not insight into essence itself. Only intuitive science penetrates to the individual.

The medium of reason is the common notions, which are *entia rationis*, as abstracted from the concrete reality of their ground. The common notion quantity both can and cannot be identified with the attribute extension, in the sense that extension both is and is not a simple idea. We know this because the *Ethic* proves that, for Spinoza, the idea of substance is both a simple and a complex idea. For Spinoza, the common notions are abstractions from an infinite, integrated real and, therefore, infinitely definable, infinitely available to increasing integration and concreteness. This is, of course, to move from common notions toward knowledge of the whole. The abstracted elements must be resolved back into the whole. Plane may be intelligible of itself, but plane is explicated by figure, and, finally, by the nature of space itself. Every concept must be returned to continuity.

Idea is an abstraction from concrete intelligence, from realized content, yet a genuinely universal common notion. Rational abstraction renders legitimate a science of emotions, though absolutely there are only individual ideas, volitions, and desires. Further, this science, as a system of rational abstractions, represents the articulation of a ground. Just as physics is made possible by the essential geometrical dynamic of extension, must not the science of emotion be resolved into the essential nature of man?

Every concept must be returned to continuity. In this sense, cause, though ultimately deriving intelligibility from *causa sui*, could be common notion. This common notion of cause would find its source in the nature of experienced agency, the generation of one adequate idea out of another. Only so could transitive causality be recognized, for the common order of nature gives only an echo the necessary connection of cause and effect. Finally, however, as the common notion cause is universal, the necessity of reason is abstract. Necessity is only fully defined by the necessary existence of God.

CHAPTER ELEVEN

ESSENCE AND IMMORTALITY

Common notions derive from the properties of attribute and infinite mode, and their linkage into system of causal explication reflects the necessary order of the divine nature. We understand bodies as kinetic quantity in infinite pattern of determinate interreaction: from extension issues motion and rest, issues the make of the whole universe. We understand ideas as generative thought in infinite pattern of determinate interreaction: from thought issues infinite intellect, issues the idea of God, the meaning of the world.

All rational knowledge grounds in the concrete universals of attribute and infinite mode. All rational knowledge is of these infinite singulars. Yet, reason knows the concretely universal by means of rational abstraction.

We have examined in detail the doctrine of common notion, because only through it can we grasp Spinoza's theory of the conceptual relation between *entia rationis* and *entia realia*. In one sense, of course, there is no relation. It is the prime concern of intellect to avoid confusing these with one another.[34]

> Here therefore particularly is it to be observed how easily we are deceived when we confuse universals with individuals, and the entities of reason and abstractions with realities.
> (schol. prop. 49, II)

> Quare hic apprime venit notandum, quam facile decipimur, quando universalia cum singularibus, & entia rationis, & abstracta cum realibus confundimus.
> (II, 135, 21)

It is of great importance that the scholium from which we take this passage, a passage portraying the epistemic dangers of confounding universals with individuals, employs the term 'essence' in two ways. The essence of idea in the abstract is that which is common to all ideas, idea as a common property. This abstract essence does not constitute the essence of any actual idea. In the actual essence, the ideaness of the idea cannot be abstracted from that which is understood.

Thus, essence can be an abstract shared property, a rational universal, or essence can be the singular meaning of a unique thing. This is so throughout the *Ethic*. We ask, for Spinoza, which is the essence of man? Is the essence of man *ens rationis* or *ens reale*?

In our treatment of common notions, we have located three relevant categories. The first is the concrete universal singular: attributes and infinite modes. The second is the abstract rational universal: the common notions. The last is the finite individual. Our account of common notion cannot compel conclusions about the essence of man, but it is only in the context of the clearest understanding of reason as universal thought and of the ontic status of the rational universals that we can begin to address the question.

The *Ethic* gives support to three possible interpretations of the essence of man:

1) Only the essence of an individual has status as *ens reale*. The essence of man, as a universal, is an *ens rationis*. This does not, of course, deny reality to God and the infinite modes. They are, for Spinoza, unquestionably individual and *entia realia*.

2) The essence of man is an *ens reale*, a true eternal individual, and individual men privative existential expressions of that one true essence.

3) Both the essences of individuals and the essence of man are *entia realia*. That reason is the medium of the understanding of type, does not necessitate the relegation of the essence of man to the realm of *entia rationis*.

We will argue that one of these interpretations is most consistent with Spinoza's vision, but the *Ethic* cannot be said to set it forth explicitly and unambiguously. Our conclusions greatly affect the details of the doctrine of immortality, but be it here said that the claim and larger significance of this doctrine are most explicit and unambiguous.

Let us state the case of the first interpretation. The *Ethic* is about reason, and reason, as we have seen, operates in terms of rational universals. Knowledge of the second kind remains universal and abstract. It deals with essence as common notion, abstracted from an infinitely concrete and integrated real. The essences of *ratio* are *entia rationis*.

Indeed, language will go no further than this—the articulation of rational type. It can only point beyond itself to actual essence, the genetic activity of eternity. Could we, then, expect the *Ethic* to give us unique essence straight? Constrained by language must it not give man as abstract type?

Further, the moral exemplar is explicitly presented as *ens rationis*.

> We desire to form for ourselves an idea of man upon which we may look as a model of human nature. (preface, IV)

> ideam hominis tanquam naturae humanae exemplar, quod intueamur, formare cupimus. (II, 208, 15)

The construction of this ideal man is intimately related to the construction of good and evil. Good and evil are 'modes of thought' (preface,
IV). At the highest level, they are ancillaries to the rational understanding of man as finite mode. We may have true knowledge of good and evil,
that is, we may genuinely understand in what the life of reason consists,
but:

> The true knowledge of good and evil which we possess is only abstract and
> universal.   (schol. prop. 62, IV)

> vera boni, et mali cognitio, quam habemus, non nisi abstracta, sive
> universalis sit.   (II, 257, 28)

Unique individuals take hold of this exemplar to steady themselves in the
flux of affective live, just as they commit to memory the *dogmata*, or 'sure
maxims of life,' and constantly apply them to particular cases (schol.
prop. 10, V).

According to our first interpretation, ideal man is a logical continua-
tion of the meaning of man in nature, but its ontic potency derives from
shared properties understood abstractly. It is an abstract idea derived
from a common essence, or *ens rationis*.

In our examination of common notions, we have judged that Spinoza's rejection of universals, in the scholium to proposition 49, part II,
pertains to rational universals. Will is described as the affirmation
common to all ideas. In a passage immediately preceding this, the
scholium to proposition 48, Spinoza writes:

> The intellect and will, therefore, are related to this or that idea or volition as
> rockiness is related to this or that rock, or as man is related to Peter or Paul.
>   (schol. prop. 48, II)

> Adeo ut intellectus, & voluntas ad hanc, & illam ideam, vel ad hanc, & illam
> volitionem eodem modo sese habeant, ac lapideitas ad hunc, & illum
> lapidem, vel ut homo ad Petrum, & Paulum.   (II, 129, 24)

In this context, his remarks would seem to support the first interpretation, indicating an abstract status for the essence of man and positing the
reality only of individuals.

Moreover, despite its necessarily typal account, much of the *Ethic*
becomes unintelligible unless read as an affirmation of the reality of the
individual. Thus, proposition 11 of part II reads:

> The first thing which forms the actual being of the human mind is nothing
> else than the idea of an individual thing actually existing.   (prop. 11, II)

> Primum, quod actuale Mentis humanae esse constituit, nihil aliud est,
> quam idea rei alicujus singularis actu existentis.   (II, 94, 14)

As the scholium to proposition 17 of part II tells us, the essence of Peter's mind explicates Peter's body. If individual essence is not reality, axiom 4, II, becomes truly problematic.

> We perceive that a certain body is affected in many ways.   (axiom 4, II)
>
> Nos corpus quoddam multis modis affici sentimus.   (II, 86, 4)

For Spinoza, it is certainly this real, experiencing individual that struggles to understand, that rejoices in its knowledge, and that transcends the phenomenal, the imaginatively constituted common order of nature. Transcendence, Spinoza demonstrates in part V, depends upon God's idea expressing the eternal essence of 'this or that' human body (prop. 22, V). The individual's realization of this essential body as unimpeded agency generates eternal mind (dem. prop. 39, V.).

A view of the immortality of the mind as purely individual seems to be supported by proposition 8 of part II and the ensuing discussion.

> The ideas of non-existent individual things or modes are comprehended in the infinite idea of God, in the same way that the formal essences of individual things or modes are contained in the attributes of God.
>   (prop. 8, II)
>
> Ideae rerum singularium, sive modorum non existentium ita debent comprehendi in Dei infinita idea, ac rerum singularium, sive modorum essentiae formales in Dei attributis continentur.   (II, 90, 32)

Individual durational existence has its individual counterpart as essence. Proposition 8, II, taken together with the statement that there is a necessary reason or cause for the non-existence as well as for the existence of anything (first additional proof prop. 11, I), portrays the eternal creativity of God as determinate infinite in which a range of individuals are occluded at the phenomenal level. Essentially the infinite is actual, the essence of each individual is contained in the attributes of God. The essence of man is an *ens rationis*. Only the essence of an individual has status as *ens reale*.

A difficult and important text for our assessment of the essence of man, we locate in the second scholium to proposition 8, part I. Here Spinoza proves from the nature of definition that there can be but one substance of the same attribute.

> The true definition of any one thing neither involves nor expresses anything except the nature of the thing defined.   (schol. 2 prop. 8, I)
>
> notandum est . . . veram uniuscujusque rei definitionem nihil involvere, neque exprimere praeter rei definitae naturam.   (II, 50, 22)

It follows from this definition of definition that no set number of instantiations can be involved. A definition involves or expresses only the nature of the thing defined. In this passage, Spinoza discusses the definitions of human nature and of triangle.

Those who follow the first interpretation and consider the essence of man a rational universal may argue that the use of triangle as an example indicates that the idea of man is *ens rationis*. Triangles are entities of reason for Spinoza. *Entia rationis* are rational abstractions from concrete and constitutive community. Spinoza talks about the essences of *entia rationis* and about *entia rationis* as the essences of things.

Is this what he means here? We must remember that Spinoza uses geometrical examples to illustrate metaphysical relationships. He does this in his account of non-existent modes in the scholium to proposition 8, part II. There, he specifically states that the model of the circle and the rectangles it comprehends is merely illustrative, since, to the metaphysical truth, there is no adequate analogy. It must be grasped directly.

We find, however, a far more weighty argument against reading this text in support to an abstract nature for human essence, an argument that, indeed, supports the opposing claim, the claim that only the essence of man is real, with men privative expressions of that essence.

In earlier chapters of this study, we have developed the contrast essence/existence in terms of unity and plurality. We have shown the relation of this theme to Spinoza's doctrine of immanent causation.

In the proof under discussion, Spinoza writes:

> We must conclude generally that whenever it is possible for several individuals of the same nature to exist, there must necessarily be an external cause for their existence.   (schol. 2 prop. 8, I)

> propterea absolute concludendum, omne id, cujus naturae plura individua existere possunt, debere necessario ut existant, causam externam habere.   (II, 51, 12)

Does this mean that if there is more than one of the same thing, we are not dealing with wholly immanent causation? If it is immanent causation, that is, causation according to the laws of its specific being, its activity self-defined, then there can be only one.

This looks like evidence for the privative nature of individual men. The 'cause for human nature generally' gives us a unique essence of man (schol. 2 proof 8, I). The essence of man is an *ens reale*, a true eternal individual, and individual men, privative existential expressions of that one true essence, our second interpretation.

The scholium to proposition 17, part I, strengthens this reading.

> One man is the cause of the existence but not of the essence of another, for the essence is an eternal truth; and therefore with regard to essence the two

men may exactly resemble one another, but with regard to existence they must differ. Consequently if the existence of one should perish, that of the other will not therefore perish; but if the essence of one could be destroyed and become false, the essence of the other would be likewise destroyed. (schol. prop. 17, I)

Homo est causa existentiae, non vero essentiae alterius hominis; est enim haec aeterna veritas: & ideo secundum essentiam prorsus convenire possunt; in existendo autem differe debent; & propterea, si unius existentia pereat, non ideo alterius peribit; sed, si unius essentia destrui posset, & fieri falsa, destrueretur etiam alterius essentia. (II, 63, 18)

Man is one in essence, many in existence.

The scholium to proposition 48, part II, which rejects man as a universal, may then be tied to Spinoza's relegation of *termini transendentales* and *notiones universales* to the realm of imagination (schol. 1 prop. 40, II). He is rejecting not a common essence, but a universal formed 'from individual cases' (schol. prop. 48, II).

Clearly, Spinoza recognizes species difference as possessing ontic import. He writes:

Hence it follows that the affects of animals which are called irrational . . . differ from human affects as much as the nature of a brute differs from that of a man. . . . The lusts and appetites of insects, fishes and birds must vary in the same way; and so, although each individual lives contented with its own nature and delights in it, nevertheless the life with which it is contented and its joy are nothing but the idea or soul of that individual, and so the joy of one differs in character from the joy of the other as much as the essence of one differs from the essence of the other. (schol. prop. 57, III)

Hinc sequitur affectus animalium, quae irrationalia dicuntur . . . ab affectibus hominum tantum differre, quantum eorum natura a natura humana differt. . . . Sic etiam Libidines, & Appetitus Insectorum, piscium, & avium alii atque alii esse debent. Quamvis itaque unumquodque individuum sua, qua constat natura, contentum vivat, eaque gaudeat, vita tamen illa, qua unumquodque est contentum, & gaudium nihil aliud est, quam idea, seu anima ejusdem individui, atque adeo gaudium unius a gaudio alterius tantum natura discrepat, quantum essentia unius ab essentia alterius differt. (II, 187, 6)

A horse is as much destroyed by being changed into a man as by being changed into an insect. Each species has its own 'essence or form' (intro., IV).

According to the second interpretation, the essence of man is the real subject of the *Ethic*, this essence under privation in the common order of nature, rule of external causation, and this essence in itself as the unimpeded agency of reason, rule of immanent causation.

> Whatever follows from human nature, in so far as it is determined by reason
> . . . , must be understood through human nature alone as through its
> proximate cause.
>   (dem. prop. 35, IV)

> quicquid ex humana natura, quatenus ratione definitur, sequitur, id . . .
> per solam humanam naturam, tanquam per proximam suam causam,
> debet intelligi.
>   (II, 223, 3)

The order of the intellect is the same in all men (schol. prop. 18, II), and
man's highest good, necessarily common to all (prop. 36, IV). In so far
as men live according to the guidance of reason, they must always agree
in nature (prop. 35, IV). Indeed, when individuals of 'exactly the same
nature' join together, they form a stronger single individual (schol. prop.
18, IV). It is only man under privation that is many.

> In so far as men are subject to passions, they cannot be said to agree in
> nature.
>   (prop. 32, IV)

> Quatenus homines passionibus sunt obnoxii, non possunt eatenus dici,
> quod natura conveniant.
>   (II, 230, 20)

Reason makes men one individual.

Reason is the postive agency of man, and the identity of anything
consists in the positive and in no sense in negation (schol. prop. 32, IV).
Passivity is submission to external determination, and man, in so far as
he suffers, is not man (props. 32-35, IV). Essential man is the true
individual, an *ens reale* as the second interpretation claimed.

We have examined evidence for the claim that only individual essences
are real and evidence for the claim that the essence of man alone is real.
In the first case, the moral exemplar is a rational universal principle for
the organization of consciousness, which is transcended by individual
insight into God's essential nature. In the latter case, the moral exemplar
is the definition of man's essence as transcendent source for durational
moral growth, the meaning of man as contained in God's essential
nature. In the first case, the realized mind of Peter or mind of Paul is the
eternal mode, and, in the latter, the singular essential mind of man
(schol. prop. 40, V).

The eternal nature of mind, for Spinoza, derives from the understanding of body under the form of eternity (prop. 29, V). Perhaps exegesis of
the proposition positing this will serve to unify these opposing views.

Before we can address this question, we must clarify the meaning of
the essence of the body. Specifically, we must ask is the essence of the
body kinetic or ideal, is it physical energy or is it idea?

The scholium to proposition 20, V, closes with the remark:

It is time, therefore, that I should now pass to consideration of those matters
which appertain to the duration of the mind without relation to the body.
                                                                (schol. prop. 20, V)

Tempus igitur jam est, ut ad illa transeam, quae ad Mentis durationem sine
relatione ad Corpus pertinent.   (II, 294, 22)

There is no doubt that Spinoza employs the term 'duration' here, not
because he wishes to claim that the mind endures without relation to the
body, but because he intends to demonstrate that the eternity of God,
known abstractly in the first part of the *Ethic*, is precisely the eternity of
the mind realized in intuitive science. The immortality of the mind is not
explained by 'duration or time, even if the duration be conceived without
beginning or end' (explan. def. 8, I; schol. prop. 23, V; dem. prop. 29,
V; schol. prop. 34, V). Immortality is man's share in the eternal nature
of God.
    Spinoza does, however, speak of the love of God as related to the mind
alone surviving the destruction of the body (schol. prop. 20, V). How
this can be, when the parallel nature of the attributes, upon which his
entire theory of transcendence turned, was grounded in their identity,
may well puzzle us.
    The transcendence of affect accomplished in the intellectual ordering
of thought finds its 'possibility,' as we have seen, in the *idea ideae*. We
might, thus, be tempted to read the immortality of mind as a kind of
'retraction' of consciousness into essence.[35] Such an interpretation could
find support in proposition 8, part II, with its geometrical analogue to
whole and existent and non-existent modes. Non-existent rectangles
exist 'merely in so far as they are comprehended in the idea of the circle'
(schol. prop. 8, II). Yet, this cannot be right, for the other side of it is a
picture of individuals 'precipitating' out of eternity, and individuals do
not precipitate out of eternity into time. Duration is not something other
than eternity. Eternity is the self-caused existence of infinite being from
which all finite existence follows. This dependence of finite upon infinite
cannot be temporal, for it is the expression of God's immanance in each
thing (schol. prop. 28, I). The absolute other of God is not absolutely
other. Yet, the finite is caused by an other, and necessarily finite other.
Contained in divine unity, the finite individual endures as determined
and determinate in a multiplicity of transactions (prop. 28, I). Thus,
finitude is a matter of perspective, the pull to lose perspective on the
whole, perspective on substance. Duration is not at a when. It is an
abstraction from the struggle of infinite finite individuals for the self-
transcendence that is being as becoming.
    We remember from our discussion of body that body means body in act,

body as potency of reagency reacting to its active complement in nature, power of response delimited by the measure of community. That the human body has in common with all bodies, is the very nature of its agency.

The less complex organism does not have enough in common to grasp its community. It has no *chance* to grasp its own meaning. The 'form of man' is man's *chance* to know himself through knowledge of community with the whole.

The essence or form of man must, then, be constituted by a specific range of community, a unity that is configuration of common properties. This essence can be expressed either as physical or as psychical force. The great emphasis of the *Ethic* is, however, on consciousness, and, in the latter part of book V, Spinoza turns his attention to pure, intrinsic mind. The mind that survives the death of the body is not the phenomenal mind, thought as imagination and passive affect. Phenomenal mind is destroyed together with phenomenal body, composite of impingement and trace (props. 21 & 34, V). The *Ethic*, part V, focuses upon the essence of body as idea, but it is able to do this because the doctrine of the attributes introduced in book I is consumated as epistemic transcendence in book V. God is one: the essence of the mind is the essence of the body.

This range of community that constitutes the eternal mode cannot be identified with substance as a whole. Spinoza is not talking about a merging of finite into infinite mind that would have the laws of extension, physical nature as a whole, as its counterpart. The essential body is not the whole of nature in the sense that substance itself is the whole of nature. It is the whole of nature, but only in a limited range of community. It is a limited pervasion of the whole. The claim that makes the whole the body is in a sense, however, correct, for it expresses the truth that essence is not place but meaning. The essence of man is continuous with meaning of the whole, but it does not exhaust that meaning.

Given this understanding of essence as community, we can see that if man is a concrete essence, this does not preclude that individual essences should also be concrete. This is the third interpretation. The essence of man is not a class, but activity as a range of community. It is not a question of whether there is one Man or many men floating in some ideal space of eternity. All individuality is resolved into community of essence.

The laws of human affection may be derived from a concrete universal, as the laws of physics are derived from the concrete universal dynamic space. Yet, the durational individual is not merely a privative expression of this universal man. The meaning of the individual is continuous with the meaning of man.

When Spinoza writes that the emotion of one individual differs from the emotion of another to the extent that they differ in essence (dem.

prop. 57, III), he is not referring to privative durational nature, but to the essential nature of the enduring individual. Men's emotions may set them in opposition to one another, but this need not mean these emotions are the only differentiating factors. We have spoken of external and immanent causation, examining an argument that denies reality to beings in so far as externally affected. We may deny a man reality in his passivity without disallowing his genuine individuation through act. The individual individuates through the clarification of community. The phenomenal body is essence conditioned by other into endurance, and the phenomenal body is transcended by the clarification of community. So far as a man grasps community through the phenomenal body, thus far does he transcend the experience of impingement, of external causation. His sorrows can become the nourishment of consciousness.

There can and, for Spinoza, must be differentiation of essence, for there to be differentiation of existence. The difference of eternity is different from the difference of duration, but not absolutely. Man's manness is not a durational matter, nor is the Peterness of Peter, the Paulness of Paul. The nature or essence of any being expresses the eternal reality of absolute act as infinite differentiation. The essences of finite individuals differ as differing affections of substance. Their meaning is essence and, hence, not intrinsically durational. Yet, the mesh of difference that is the divine order determines them again and yet again into the experience of duration. The immanence of God is essence, but finite essence cannot cause existence. Finite existence finds genesis in the nexus of interdetermination that is the causal efficacy of substance. Eternity is infinite community of essence as source of difference.

Spinoza may speak of a form of man which can be made an authentic ethical telos, because of the essential nature of those purposing to become themselves. The moral exemplar is not final cause, but abstract representation of efficient causation. The essence of man is the concrete complex of community and difference that defines men. Individual men recognize in this real essence the form of their transcendence, the form of reason as human inseity. Spinoza may also speak of unique individuals striving for adequate knowledge (dem. prop. 1, III).

The scholium to proposition 57, part III, cited earlier as giving ontic import to species difference, sees essence as not only characteristic of type, but also as unique to various individuals.

> Although each individual lives contented with its own nature and delights in it, nevertheless the life with which it is contended and its joy are nothing but the idea or soul of that individual, and so the joy of one differs in character from the joy of the other as much as the essence of the one differs from the essence of the other. (schol. prop. 57, III)

> Quamvis itaque unumquodque individuum sua, qua constat natura, con-
> tentum vivat, eaque gaudeat, vita tamen illa, qua unumquodque est
> contentum, & guadium nihil aliud est, quam idea, seu anima ejusdem
> individui, atque adeo gaudium unius a gaudio alterius tantum natura
> discrepat, quantum essentia unius ab essentia alterius differt. (II, 187, 12)

Thus does the enslaving joy of the drunkard differ from the freeing joy of
the philosopher (schol. prop. 57, III). Each individual struggles to
approximate to an eternal limit of self, to realize an intrinsic potency of
immanent causation. For all men, this is done through immanent
causation as adequate knowledge. In this sense, reason is the form of
man, and the knowledge of God that is its end is common to all men, for:

> Man could not be nor be conceived if he had not the power of rejoicing in
> this highest good.   (schol. prop. 36, IV)

> homo nec esse, nec concipi posset, si potestatem non haberet gaudendi hoc
> summo bono.   (II, 235, 7)

The affective life that brings disunity to men likewise brings disunity to
self (prop. 33, IV). In the common order of nature, all essence is, in one
sense, at risk. Mind unifies itself as essence. Through unification with
nature, it transcends its partiality, becomes unified according to the
order of the intellect. As men become one, the individual becomes itself
one. Indeed, only by becoming more oneself does one become man.

In the *Ethic*, Spinoza does not fully articulate the status of rational
universals in relation to the essence of man. Within the text, it is difficult
always to distinguish between the false universals of imagination,
rejected outright, and the true universals of reason, efficacy limited by
their abstract nature.

We believe correct the reading of the *Ethic* accepting both the essence
of man and the essences of men as *entia realia*. Thought may legitimately
abstract from essence, as in natural science and as in the construction of
the moral exemplar, but, for Spinoza, all actual essence is concrete. The
ens realissimum contains all essence.

For Spinoza, to be comprehended in the divine attributes is to be real.
Entia rationis are abstract modes of thought. They are not false, but
neither are they fully true: they are inadequate expressions of the
concrete nature of substance. By individual, Spinoza means concrete
essence.

Thus, while Spinoza posits the existence only of the individual, we
think it inaccurate to term him a nominalist. He certainly rejects the
imaginal universals embodied in most discourse, the universals of sign
and inconstant experience (schol. 2 prop. 40, II). As we have seen, he

also denies ultimate reality to abstract rational universals. Nevertheless, there remain elements of genuine universality without which his philosophy becomes unintelligible.[36]

The attributes are concrete universals, as are the infinite modes. Proximate causes of all being, there follow from them infinite things in infinite ways. Here, the parallel order and connection of the modes represents a further aspect of the universality of pervasion by divine essence. God is Himself absolute universal, the universal origin of all dependent things.

The necessity of the divine nature creates infinitely the infinite continuum of essence. This necessity, grasped abstractly, we know as the laws of logic/nature. This continuum of essence, we know abstractly as the common notions. In this sense, are the attributes the forms of things, as cause of their content.

Like Plato, Spinoza is talking about causes. Spinoza did not speak in Plato's language, but he was likewise a realist. This comparison cannot, of course, be developed or substantiated here, nor do we suggest that intertranslation yields commensurability without contrast.[37] At the conclusion of this study, Spinoza's unique contribution to the realist tradition will be considered.

We have argued that Spinoza possesses a doctrine of type, of concrete essences common to a plurality of individuals. It is fair to say that, in the *Ethic*, his doctrine of type is not fully achieved. For the reader, as, we believe, for Spinoza, questions remain.

Given the essential reality of man and of men, how would Spinoza apply the principle of reciprocity of essence and existence? How would he relate the notion of several orders of individuality to his account of the weaving of infinite intellect out of individual eternal modes (schol. prop. 40, V)? In response to these queries, we can do no more than reiterate our explication of community and continuity.

In conclusion, we must examine the proposition in which, together with its scholium, we find the only occurence in the *Ethic*, or in the entire corpus of Spinoza's works, of the term *forma hominis*, the form of man.

> The Being of substance does not pertain to the essence of man, or, in other words, substance does not constitute the form of man.   (prop. 10, II)

> Ad essentiam hominis non pertinet esse substantiae, sive substantia formam hominis non constituit.   (II, 92, 28)

This proposition posits the modal nature of man, his total dependence upon substance. Man is not himself a substance. His being does not involve necessary existence.

In its context, immediately following the proposition defining finite determination (prop. 9, II), proposition 10 clearly pertains to the actually existing mode. Does it hold for eternal man, for the mind as eternal mode of thought?

> Our mind, in so far as it understands, is an eternal mode of thought, which is determined by another eternal mode of thought, and this again by another, and so *ad infinitum*. So that all taken together form the eternal and infinite intellect of God. (schol. prop. 40, V)
>
> Mens nostra, quatenus intelligit, aeternus cogitandi modus sit, qui alio aeterno cogitandi modo determinatur, & hic iterum ab alio, & sic in infinitum; ita ut omnes simul Dei aeternum, & infinitum intellectum constituant. (II, 306, 21)

We answer, substance does not constitute the form of man, either as enduring or as eternal being. Here, we may clarify our understanding of the doctrine of immanent causation.

The consequences of this doctrine in the second scholium to proposition 8, I, were employed in an argument for the ontic legitimacy of the essence of man. There, immanent causation was identified with unity, and the reality of a plurality of individuals of the same nature denied. The identification of immanent causation with the intrinsic power of the individual, its oneness, is certainly correct. In that context, however, immanent causation is identified absolutely with *causa sui*, and, thus, unity is identified with necessary existence.

For Spinoza, that something exists as itself is a function of immanent causation. A thing is itself in so far as it enacts its essence. Existence follows from essence, but only under the rule of God's infinite causal efficacy.

> God is not only the efficient cause of the existence of things, but also of their essence. (prop. 25, I)
>
> Deus non tantum est causa efficiens rerum existentiae, sed etiam essentiae. (II, 67, 27)

The immanent causation of each thing, in one sense is, and in another is not, the immanent causation of God. The potency of each being dependent upon God is internal to it, but no thing dependent upon God can be absolutely identified with *causi sui*. Necessary existence belongs only to the divine nature.

The scholium to proposition 10, part II, repeating this argument for the necessary existence of the absolutely one, confirms our understanding of dependent existence.

Mind as eternal mode remains dependent upon God. The infinitude and eternity of the infinite modes is necessary because of its cause (dem.

prop. 21, I). Spinoza speaks of the complex of eternal modes as the infinite intellect of God (schol. prop. 40, V), and the infinite intellect 'must be referred to the *natura naturata* and not to the *natura naturans*' (prop. 31, I). Substance transcends its expression in modal nature.

That substance does not constitute the form of man means that the mode may not endure. No individual in nature cannot be overpowered by a more powerful other (ax., IV). No finite being cannot encounter in its others dissoulution and death. Elsewhere, we have read the over- whelming and fragmented realm of sense as image of the whole's transcendence of its parts. The finite individual may fail to assimilate its experience. Thus is the risk of destruction the form of divine transcen- dence at the phenomenal level. Yet, even at the level of the eternal modes, God's transcendence remains absolute.

Eternal by God's eternity, the infinite modes cannot be destroyed. The intellectual love of God is the love with which He loves Himself (prop. 36, V), a love infinite and eternal. The axiom of the fourth part refers only to the phenomenal, to the dimension of durational existence (schol. prop. 37, V).

> There is nothing in nature which is contrary to this intellectual love, or which can negate it.   (prop. 37, V)

> Nihil in natura datur, quod huic Amori intellectuali sit contrarium, sive quod ipsum possit tollere.   (II, 303, 27)

Durational man is essence under privation, but privation known as plenitude under the aspect of eternity. Through the realization of community of essence, man transcends the phenomenal self to accede to union with the truth rejoicing in itself. He becomes a part of the mind of God. He is fully God, but only in so far as God can be manifested through the essence of the human mind (prop. 36, V).

Divine immanence is the unity, the creativity, of each individual. Yet, as Spinoza insists, every one is infinitely transcended by the one of God, by the infinite creativity of being by definition.

CONCLUSION

As Spinoza's doctrine of essence is an exploration of the problem of the one and the many, preeminently of the ethical implications of the one and the many for a finite being, it is not surprising to conclude that the *Ethic* does not offer an exhaustive account of man's essential nature.

Yet, in its potent complexity, we recognize the form of man. The *Ethic* gives us the form of man and the demand for its realization in the knowledge of God.

The *Ethic* is the idea of Being, and it demands being. For the durational individual, being is becoming, and the possibility of transcendence is the paradox of growth.

The resistance to change characterizes the enduring organism, both in so far as it is self according to its own order of being and in so far as it is self deformed by the mark of the other. Mind perseveres both in so far as it has adequate and inadequate ideas.

> The mind, both in so far as it has clear and distinct ideas, and in so far as it has confused ideas, endeavours to persevere in its being for an indefinite time, and is conscious of this effort. (prop. 9, III)

> Mens tam quatenus claras, & distinctas quam quatenus confusas habet ideas, conatur in suo esse perseverare indefinita quadam duratione, & hujus sui conatus est conscia. (II, 147, 15)

Growth is possible because *conatus* expresses essence as a power to assimilate experience. The immutable eternal form of the individual is its power to live, the rule of its survival over against that which would fragment and destroy it.

Only in so far as the individual remains one has it the power to grow. Here, the resistance to change is the power to change. In so far as the resistance takes the form accorded the individual by the common order of nature, the resistance to change is the refusal of growth.

In the measure that his past defines him, man denies the power by which he may transcend. His joy is the mixed, irrational joy of the composite phenomenal self.

We have seen that the mind's object is both the body and encountered other, that, for the experiencing individual, all things are the body as world. The individual is his desire for the joy of the body, and he knows every person or thing in terms of its enhancement of the body's joy (props. 12 & 13, III). The composite individual desires to preserve the joy it knows, or, more accurately, imagines. It struggles to preserve this phenomenal soul.

The object of the phenomenal mind is, in this sense, the past, the body as association of impingements. Spinoza writes in the scholium to proposition 36, III, of *desiderium*, longing, as a sadness of frustrated desire, the frustrated desire that pleasure should always be the same.

> He who recollects a thing with which he has once been delighted, desires to possess it with every condition which existed when he was first delighted with it.   (prop. 36, III)

> Qui rei, qua semel delectatus est, recordatur, cupit eadem cum iisdem potiri circumstantiis, ac cum primo ipsa delectatus est.   (II, 167, 29)

We long for the past as itself a complex object of desire.

Man's moral choice is between the past and eternity.

Man, believing himself this conditioned consciousness, fears change as loss of self. He cannot but be frustrated in his desire for sameness of pleasure. Only eternity is pleasure always the same. The eternal and infinite object nourishes with unmixed joy, strengthening man's generosity and courage (schol. prop. 59, III). In direct knowledge of being, the free man ceases to fear death (prop. 67, IV & prop. 38, V).

We have earlier examined Spinoza's conception of the mind's eternity and the transcendence of durational existence. It is instructive that the proposition immediately following Spinoza's demonstration of the potency of intuitive science in access to God's immutable and eternal love concerns the nature of the durational body.

> He who possesses a body fit for many things possesses a mind of which the greater part is eternal.   (prop. 39, V)

> Qui Corpus ad plurima aptum habet, is Mentem habet, cujus maxima pars est aeterna.   (II, 304, 33)

Here, Spinoza posits the complexity of the human body as proof of the eternity of the mind (schol. prop. 39, V). This is the deeply original claim of the *Ethic*: the meaning of the durational body is the eternity of the mind. We know no other philosopher who has conceived so seriously the body's truth.

Spinoza's insistence upon the status of extension as divine attribute is continuous with his emphasis on the body's significance for cognition. He manifests the meaning of body as consciousness.

Further, he is faithful to our experience of body. We read in his logic of passional life the true sense of our joys and sorrows. His account of transcendence distorts no detail of durational sufferance.

Spinoza has understood the union of mind and body as mind's knowledge of body. In the *Short Treatise on God, Man and His Well-Being*, he describes this knowledge as love, writing, 'Even the knowledge that we have of the body is not such that we know it just as it is, or perfectly; and yet, what a union! what a love!'[38] The *Ethic* gives full account of that love or potency of union.

In the earlier work, Spinoza calls for transcendence of the body as mutable object. Through increasing knowledge of God, the individual achieves union with Him. Man turns from love of the body to love of God and attains union with an immutable object.

We suggest that the more mature *Ethic* has transformed this account by making transcendence not a turning away from body to God, but an opening out of the body's meaning into eternal being.[39] We have a movement through, rather than a turning from. Our union with God is the enjoyment of eternity in mind's conception of the eternal essence of the body (prop. 30, V). We transcend by truly knowing the body. Thus is the durational body no lie, but our initiation into the order of essence.

We see, in the *Ethic*'s austere *speculum mundi*, the play of fortune and the reality of God. Man in nature suffers God's reality as fortune, but man may come to know in fortune the reality of God.

In pain and aging, the body teaches us the meaning of fate. It is Spinoza's great genius that he has shown us in this *memento mori* our opening into eternal life.

NOTES

1. For a good discussion of the historical context of the *natura naturans/natura naturata* distinction, see Martial Gueroult, *Spinoza*, I, (Paris: Montaigne, 1968), pp. 564–68.

2. We argue that for Spinoza the concepts unity and infinitude entail one another. In the context of a comparison between Bruno and Spinoza, Arturo Derigibus considers the problem of the unity of the infinite in Spinoza's philosophy. Deregibus offers an account of the multiplicity necessary to unity. Of particular interest is his analysis of Spinoza's thought in terms of the transformation of Copernicanism by the assimilation of the idea of the infinite. See Arturo Deregibus, *La dottrina di Spinoza sull'infinito*, Vol. II of *Bruno e Spinoza; la realtà dell'infinito e il problema della sua unità* (Turin: Giappichelli, 1981).

3. See Ep. 12, *The Correspondence of Spinoza*, ed. A. Wolf (London: George Allen & Unwin, 1928), pp. 114–22. An excellent exegesis of this letter is Martial Gueroult's 'Spinoza's Letter on the Infinite,' in *Spinoza*, ed. Marjorie Grene (Garden City: Doubleday 1973), pp. 182–212. For an important proof of the unreality of number in the *Ethic*, see also Gilles Deleuze, *Spinoza et le problème de l'expression* (Paris: Éditions de Minuit, 1968), pp. 21–32. The denial of many substances of the same attribute and of many substances of different attribute means that no real distinction is numeric and no numeric distinction is real.

4. This study does not employ the term 'pantheism' to describe Spinoza's philosophy. While the *Pantheismusstreit* was important for the history of Spinoza scholarship, the term 'pantheism' is itself ambiguous and not inherently useful. As John Hunt notes in *An Essay on Pantheism*, 'Of the word Pantheism we have no fixed definition. The most opposite beliefs are sometimes called by this name.' See John Hunt, *An Essay on Pantheism*, rev. ed. (London: Gibbings, 1893), p. 1.

   The term 'pantheism' may thus be used to cover diverse interpretations of Spinoza. Victor Delbos, for example, refers Spinoza's pantheism to divine infinity and to the nature that unites a heterogeneity of being overcoming the dualism of thinking and extended substance. See Victor Delbos, 'La notion de substance et la notion de dieu dans las philosophie de Spinoza,' in *Revue de métaphysique et de morale* (No. 6, 1908), 783–88. In contrast, William F. Cooley sees in the pantheism of Spinoza (as also in that of Plotinus) a quantitative view of perfection. See William F. Cooley, 'Spinoza's Pantheistic Argument,' in *Studies in the History of Ideas* (New York: Columbia U., 1918) pp. 171–87.

   Similarly, a definition of pantheism may be constructed and used to affirm or deny Spinoza's pantheism. John Dewey describes Spinoza as a pantheist because in his system, 'God becomes the Absolute, and Nature and Self are but his manifestations.' See John Dewey, 'The Pantheism of Spinoza,' in the *Journal of Speculative Philosophy*, 16 (1882), 249–57. Harry Austryn Wolfson argues that if Spinoza's conception of the relation of God to world is to be described as pantheism, it is pantheism with a difference, in order to distinguish it from a pantheism positing that all beings are of the essence or nature of God as in John Scotus Erigena or Amalric of Bena. See H. A. Wolfson, *The Philosophy of Spinoza*, II (1934; New York: rpt. Schocken, 1969), pp. 38–39.

   By some commentators, the term 'pantheism' is rejected and another term preferred. Martial Gueroult rejects the term 'pantheism,' because Spinoza thinks not that everything is God, but that everything is in God. Gueroult prefers the term 'panentheism.' See M. Gueroult, *Spinoza*, I (Paris: Montaigne, 1968), p. 223. Frederick Kettner prefers the term 'hentheism,' because the all constitutes one totality. See Frederick Kettner, *Spinoza The Biosopher* (New York: Roerich Museum Press, 1932), p. 140.

Other commentators question or reject the term 'pantheism,' because they do not regard Spinoza as a theist. William F. Cooley utilizes the term 'pantheist,' but sees in the quantitative pantheism of Spinoza a voiding of the religious associations of a personal theism. See 'Spinoza's Pantheistic Argument.' James Martineau argues that, by Kant's definition of theism, Spinoza ought be viewed atheist. See James Martineau, *A Study of Spinoza* (London: Macmillan, 1882).

It is precisely with regard to the alleged 'atheism' of Spinoza that the pantheism controversy was important. As debate concerning Spinoza's pantheism has been avoided here, so likewise that concerning his theism or atheism. These are strong words, significant for understanding the response to Spinoza's philosophy, but not deeply useful for elucidating the philosophy itself.

While the varying readings of Spinoza's pantheism presented here do not find place within equally valid interpretations of Spinoza, they serve to illustrate problems with use of the term. That the term may, in fact, be effectively utilized in exposition of Spinoza is witnessed by Richard Avenarius's classic study of the development of Spinoza's thought. See Richard Avenarius, *Ueber die beiden ersten Phasen des Spinozischen Pantheismus und das Verhältniss der zweiten zur dritten Phase* (Leipzig: E. Avenarius, 1868).

We have preferred to focus on divine 'immanence,' an immanence Gilles Deleuze describes as '*univocité*,' in his study that most correctly denies the ascription of either a creationist or an emanationist account of the relation of God to all things in the *Ethic*. See G. Deleuze, *Spinoza et le problème de l'expression* (Paris: Éditions de Minuit, 1968), pp. 153–69.

5.   For a profound reading of Spinoza's conception of duration, see Harold Foster Hallett, *Aeternitas* (Oxford: Clarendon Press, 1930). Jonathan Bennett, in his *A Study of Spinoza's Ethics* (Indianapolis: Hackett, 1984), raises a number of logical questions concerning Spinoza's theory of time, interesting for their demands on our comprehension of motion and rest. See pages 193–211. Bennett's discussion is, however, rendered problematic by an understanding of eternity inimical to ours.

6.   Important texts for Spinoza's discussion of causality and definition are Ep. 9, *The Correspondence of Spinoza*, ed. A. Wolf (London: George Allen & Unwin, 1928), pp. 105–09, and *On the Improvement of the Understanding*, in *Spinoza Selections*, ed. John Wild New York: Charles Scribner's Sons, 1958), pp. 36 ff. or *Spinoza Opera*, ed. Gebhardt, II, 34, 8.

7.   See Ep. 60, *The Correspondence of Spinoza*, ed. A. Wolf (London: George Allen & Unwin, 1928), pp. 300–03.

8.   See Martial Gueroult, *Spinoza*, I (Paris: Montaigne, 1968), pp. 172–75. See also Herman De Dijn, 'Historical Remarks on Spinoza's Theory of Definition,' in *Spinoza on Knowing, Being and Freedom* (Assen: Van Gorcum & Company, 1974), pp. 41–50. De Dijn's article on the influence of Hobbes and Heereboord on Spinoza's theory of definition develops in an interesting way the relation of causality and definition. The full treatment of Spinoza's notions of the complex and the simple called for by an investigation of the one and the many must be ruled beyond the limitations of our study.

9.   For a provocative discussion of this double causal relation see G. H. R. Parkinson, 'On the Power and Freedom of Man,' *The Monist*, 55, no. 4 (1971), 527–53. Evelyn Burg, in an unpublished essay, 'On Spinoza's Conceptions of Power and Freedom' (1978), offers an important critique of Parkinson's analysis of action and individual.

10. For a succinct treatment of the universals and transcendentals, see Martial Gueroult, *Spinoza*, II (Paris: Aubier-Montaigne, 1974), pp. 370–72.

11. Imagination is not a faculty, but an operation of the mind concerned with inadequate ideas. We write of universals formed 'in' or 'by' the imagination, but this is abstraction from concrete perceptions. See the scholium to proposition 48, part II.

12. cf. the *Cogitata Metaphysica*, I, chapter 6, discussion of unity in *The Principles of Descartes' Philosophy*, trans. Halbert Hains Britan (Chicago: Open Court, 1905), p. 131. See also Ep. 50, in *The Correspondence of Spinoza*, ed. A. Wolf (London: George Allen & Unwin, 1928), pp. 269–70, for rejection of 'one' as divine appellation.

13. Interpretation of Spinoza's theory of the attributes of substance has long been a sphere of contention in the critical literature. The relation of attribute to substance, the character and number of the attributes, have all been subject to debate.

Spinoza's correspondence already suggests the difficulties his attributes of substance will occasion. De Vries (Eps. 9 & 10), Schuller and the acute Tschirnhaus (Eps. 63, 64, 65, 66, 70) find problems in this doctrine.

The central issue is clearly the relation of attribute to substance, with the two basic positions traditionally designated the subjective and the objective interpretations of attribute.

The subjective largely turns on the *Ethic's* definition of attribute as that which intellect apprehends of substance as constituting its essence (def. 4, I), with much made of the translation of *tanquam* as 'as' or 'as if.' The ninth epistle's account of intellect's attribution of attribute to substance is also called upon.

J. E. Erdmann is often cited as proponent of the subjective interpretation by commentators reviewing the controversy and as often criticized for Kantianizing Spinoza, despite his disputation of the charge. See Johann Eduard Erdmann, *Grundriss der Geschichte der Philosophie*, II (Berlin: Wilhelm Hertz, 1870) pp. 56–57. Erdmann is criticized, for example, by James Martineau in *A Study of Spinoza* (London: Macmillan, 1882), p. 184, and by A. Wolf in his introduction to *The Correspondence of Spinoza* (London: George Allen & Unwin, 1928), pp. 58–59, and in his 'Spinoza's Conception of the Attributes of Substance,' in *Studies in Spinoza: Critical and Interpretive Essays*, ed. S. Paul Kashap (Berkeley: University of California Press, 1972), p. 17. According to Erdmann, Spinoza did not regard the attributes as objective characters of substance, but only as our ways of conceiving it. Another proponent of the subjective reading, Wilhelm Windelband, in *A History of Philosophy*, calls the attributes the 'two highest universal conceptions' beyond which we find *ens realissimum* as *ens generalissimum*, 'the empty Form of substance' devoid of definite content, the deity as nothing. See Wilhelm Windelband, *A History of Philosophy*, trans. James H. Tufts, 2nd ed. (New York: Macmillan, 1901), pp. 408–09.

The most important advocate of the subjective interpretation may well be Harry Austryn Wolfson. In *The Philosophy of Spinoza* (1934; New York: rpt. Schocken, 1969), Wolfson grounds his subjectivistic reading of Spinoza in the theories of divine attributes propounded by mediaeval Jewish philosophers. See Vol. I, pp. 142–57. Wolfson further regards the subjective nature of the attributes as the deductive consequence of Spinoza's nominalist theory of universals (Vol. I, pp. 152–53), but S. Gram Moltke in 'Spinoza, Substance, and Predication,' *Theoria*, 34 (1968), 222–44, has demonstrated the relation of attribute to substance independent of the ontological status of the common properties.

Wolfson's identification of substance with the *summum genus*, in the context of which he develops his reading of attribute, has been ably criticized by E. M. Curley in *Spinoza's Metaphysics* (Cambridge, Mass.: Harvard University Press, 1969), pp. 28–36. Wolfson's view of essential attributes is inseparable from his conclusion that Spinoza's God is unknowable in His essence (Vol. I, p. 142 & p. 76).

Harold Henry Joachim's *A Study of the Ethics of Spinoza* (New York: Russell & Russell, 1964), while examining difficulties of interpretation (p. 102 ff.), posits an objectivistic reading of the attributes. According to Joachim, attributes are the 'ultimate characters of Reality' (p. 22). They are irreducible one to the other, and each wholly expresses what substance is (p. 22 & p. 26).

Here, however, the role of intellect in knowing divine essence as the diverse attributes brings to the fore an awareness that readings of attribute may not be so definitely divided into subjective and objective interpretations. No interpretation denies that it is intellect that knows substance as attribute. If there is a necessary dichotomy between attribute constituting the essence of substance and attribute existing only for the knowing intellect, even objectivists are drawing the lines in different ways. Differing views concerning the unity of God, the identity and diversity of the attributes with respect to intellect, determine various strongly objectivist interpretations.

A. Wolf, rejecting Windelband's view of Spinoza as mathematical pantheist, and the logico-mathematical reading of attributes that has characterized much English Spinoza scholarship, develops a dynamic interpretation of the attributes as energy, the forces of infinite being. The infinitude of substance, Wolf regards equivalent to its completeness. Infinite means 'all' not 'innumerable.' Wolf thus concludes that there may be, but need not be, attributes other than thought and extension. For Wolf, Spinoza conceives substance identical to the totality of attributes. See 'Spinoza's Conception of the Attributes of Substance,' in *Studies in Spinoza*, ed. Kashap, pp. 16–42.

H. F. Hallett, on the other hand, while also seeing in Spinoza a dynamic philosophy of agency, grounds his theory of the attributes in a doctrine of the indeterminacy of substance. Thought and extension cannot be all the attributes. An absolutely indeterminate infinite potency necessitates an infinity of attributes. See Harold Foster Hallett's *Aeternitas* (Oxford: Clarendon Press, 1930), pp. 281–300, and his *Creation, Emanation and Salvation* (The Hague: Martinus Nijhoff, 1962), p. 47, note 2. Further, the indeterminacy of substance is the identity of the attributes, which are distinguished only from the standpoint of intellect. Itself a determinate actualization of primordial indeterminate potency, intellect conceives its source as infinite determination, infinite equivalent forms of one real. See *Creation, Emanation and Salvation*, pp. 45–51.

Finally, Francis S. Haserot, having dismantled the subjective reading through all permutations of possible translation of definition 4, I, implicitly relegates all interpretations of Spinoza that deny distinction of attributes to the subjectivist view. The attributes as 'distinct but inherent and mutually inseparable characters of substance' are the necessary metaphysical basis of determinism. See F. S. Haserot, 'Spinoza's Definition of Attribute,' in *Studies in Spinoza*, ed. Kashap, pp. 28–42.

All three, Wolf, Hallett, and Haserot emphasize the power of intellect to know the real, that is, none take the subject's participation in knowing as rendering knowledge subjective in either a pejorative or Kantian sense. Indeed, the more properly subjective interpretations seem, as a rule, to be allied to the denial that God can be known, as in Windelband and Wolfson. Lewis Robinson argues that the subjectivist interpretation of the attributes results in a God unknowable even to Himself, a position beyond even Kantian idealism. See Lewis Robinson, *Kommentar zu Spinozas Ethik* (Leipzig: Felix Meiner, 1928), p. 66.

Moltke, in his article 'Spinoza, Substance, and Predication,' analyzes the subjective and objective interpretations of attribute, and introduces a third, the linguistic. Based on the ninth epistle's remarks on name and referent, it is really a variation on the subjective. At its most extreme, the linguistic interpretation will carry us to William Thomas Jones, who describes substance as 'whatever-can-be-said' with the attributes like the various languages, each expressing 'whatever-can-be-said.' See William Thomas Jones, *A History of Western Philosophy*, (New York: Harcourt, Brace and World, Vol. III, 1952), p. 205.

Moltke rejects all three of these traditions of interpretation, arguing that the distinction of substance and attribute assumes the viability of essential predication. He attempts to show that all three positions end in contradiction. Moltke's critique, however, as a critique of Spinoza, appears troubled by misapprehension of questions concerning number and identity in Spinoza's philosophy.

Were we to be aligned with any one of the commentators discussed, our position would be closest to that of Hallett. The identity of the attributes is basic to our thesis. We are not bound, however, to argue the indeterminacy of substance, but focus, rather, on Spinoza's epistemology as an ontological claim concerning divine unity and complexity.

14.   See Harold Foster Hallett, *Benedict de Spinoza, the Elements of his Philosophy* (London: Athlone Press, 1957), p. 32, note 2, for his remarks on the translation of *facies totius universi*.

15.   The absence of a complete Spinozistic physics puts in question the status of Spinoza's *corpora simplicissima*. Are they introduced as *entia rationis* or *entia realia*? The *corpora simplicissima* demand assessment in terms of every aspect of Spinoza's doctrine on the infinite.

Stuart Hampshire, finding in Spinoza's doctrine of the *corpora simplicissima* an anticipation of the concepts and theoretical methods of modern science, sees in the simplest bodies ultimate or elementary particles as centers of energy out of which all things are composed. They are physically actual. See Stuart Hampshire, *Spinoza* (New York: Penguin, 1951), pp. 72–73, 79. Harold Henry Joachim posits in other terms the physical actuality of the simplest bodies, developing an account of individual as mere aggregate of elementary corpuscles. See H. H. Joachim, *A Study of the Ethics of Spinoza* (New York: Russell and Russell, 1964), pp. 130–31. This leads to his claim that only the *corpora simplicissima* and God are individuals in a strict sense. See *Study*, p. 141, note 3. He fails to see the role of integration in Spinoza's theory of individuality, that the doctrine of immanent causation involves always a principle of assimilation in its tension with the conative divergence of infinitely many individuals.

Harold Foster Hallett criticizes Joachim's atomistic reading, demonstrating that the simplest bodies are entity only in so far as integrated into the *facies totius universi*. Abstracted from infinite motion and rest, the simplest bodies are *entia rationis*. Hallett sees the role of the *corpora simplicissima* in the *Ethic* as ideal starting point for synthesis. The result of corporeal analysis, and not mathematical division, the simplest bodies are not unextended *puncta*. They are not the place at which the infinite and eternal is pulverized into the absolutely finite and instantaneous: there is no point at which division renders being non-being. The simplest bodies are, then, according to Hallett, 'the least of eternal things.' Their actuality is infinitesimal duration. They are necessarily unidentifiable, 'for since there can be no minimal duration, no atomic moment, it follows that there can be no *corpus simplex*.' See Harold Foster Hallett, *Aeternitas* (Oxford: Clarendon, 1930), pp. 137–41. Hence, the *corpora simplicissima*, as least complex bodies, must serve a theoretical function in the discursus on the body.

David R. Lachterman, in an excellent article on the physics of the *Ethic*, sets aside debate on the physical character of the simplest bodies, concluding that Spinoza introduces them as '"theoretical entities" whose main, if not unique explanatory burden is to anchor subsequent complex systems to the most elementary features of entities devoid of complexity and exhibiting distinctiveness only *via* their immediately comprehensible relations of motion and rest.' For Spinoza's purpose in the discursus, they are *entia rationis*. They function in the physical science by meeting certain criteria, such as fulfillment of the Cartesian law of inertia. See D. R. Lachterman, 'The Physics of Spinoza's Ethics,' in *Spinoza; New Perspectives* ed. R. W. Shahan and J. I. Biro (Norman, OK: University of Oklahoma Press, 1978), p. 84.

We believe that Hallett's and Lachterman's accounts can be correlated, with Lachterman's claims for the functional criteria of the *corpora simplicissima* defining the analytic end-point of integration into the complex of natural laws, or the *facies totius universi*.

Lachterman notes that Spinoza does not refer to any simplest body as 'individuum' or 'unum corpus.' The *corpora simplicissima* are always in the plural. If these simplest bodies are *entia rationis*, it makes no sense for us to ask of the number that form a body, how many? If they are *entia realia*, we would conclude that they must be infinite.

This is the position of Gilles Deleuze, who holds the *corpora simplicissima* infinitely small extensive parts. See Gilles Deleuze, *Spinoza et le problème de l'expression* (Paris: Éditions de Minuit, 1968), pp. 183–96. The elegant and vital interpretation of Spinoza that is the context of Deleuze's claim cannot be examined here. He develops existence as plurality in a manner relevant to its treatment in our study.

Lachterman sees Deleuze's reading as compatible with the infinite modal divisibility of substance. Lachterman, p. 107. If Hallett is correct, however, the infinite divisibility of substance bears a problematic relation to the *corpora simplicissima*.

We incline toward the view that every individual incorporates an infinite number of simplest bodies. Indeed, it would seem that if the parts of an individual were denumerable, imagination would not be continuous with reason.

We have argued in our study that the incommensurability of number with the real and the irreducibility of a thing to its parts are identical expression of the absolute concreteness of being. Does this necessitate infinite *corpora simplicissima*?

If the simplest bodies are 'the least of eternal things,' then they can be described as possessed of minimal essence. In themselves, they are almost entirely existence. This is perhaps a dangerously metaphoric way of speaking. Here, we see it necessary to relate the interpretation of the simplest bodies to Spinoza's statement in the second scholium to proposition 8, part I, about the external causality required for the existence of a number of individuals of the same kind. In that scholium, it is precisely the denumerability of individuals that tells us they are not caused by their essence. Asking, how many *corpora simplicissima* are there? we find ourselves asking, how many men are there? Number is always abstraction.

16. cf. the Ep. 32 discussion of *cohaerentia*, the cohesion or coherence among the body's parts, in *The Correspondence of Spinoza*, ed. A. Wolf (London: George Allen & Unwin, 1928), pp. 209–14.

17. For a lucid interpretation of the meaning of bodily integrity in the discursus on body, see Hans Jonas, 'Spinoza and the Theory of Organism,' in *Spinoza*, ed. Marjorie Grene (Garden City: Doubleday, 1937), pp. 259–78.

18. I am deeply indebted to the work of Harold Foster Hallett for clarification of the meaning of body in Spinoza. For a concise account, see H. F. Hallett, 'On a Reputed Equivoque in the Philosophy of Spinoza,' in *Studies in Spinoza*, ed. S. Paul Kashap (Berkeley: University of California, 1972), pp. 168–88.

19. Harold Foster Hallett introduces the term 'vigilance' to describe the bodily counterpart of consciousness. See H. F. Hallett, *Aeternitas*, (Oxford: Clarendon Press, 1930), p. 265.

20. cf. Ep. 58 discussion of the stone's 'free will,' in *The Correspondence of Spinoza*, ed. A. Wolf (London: George Allen & Unwin, 1928) pp. 295–96.

21. It is in light of this necessarily intentional character of consciousness that we may offer a critique of Descartes' *cogito* and of the Cartesian epistemology.

22. Belief in the necessary adequacy of the *idea ideae* has led commentators into difficulty. For example, Thomas Carson Mark, in his otherwise sound account of Spinoza's theory of truth, misreads the meaning of body in Spinoza. Mark's overly interior interpretation of truth largely derives from his understanding of the *idea ideae*. See Thomas Carson Mark, *Spinoza's Theory of Truth* (New York: Columbia University Press, 1972). The claim concerning *idea ideae* is made on page 64. Mark modifies his views about knowledge of extended modes in a later article. See T. C. Mark, 'Truth and Adequacy in Spinozistic Ideas,' in *Spinoza: New Perspectives*, ed. R. W. Shanan and J.I. Biro (Norman, OK: University of Oklahoma Press, 1978), pp. 11–34. Alan Hart, likewise, takes ideas of ideas to be adequate, following T. C. Mark and Daisie Radner. See Alan Hart, *Spinoza's Ethics: a Platonic Commentary* (Leiden: E. J. Brill, 1983), p. 119. We believe proposition 9, part III, proof that ideas of ideas are not necessarily adequate. The mind's consciousness of itself may be mutilated and confused.

23. We recognize in Melvin Konner's account of an experiment on plasticity of ocular dominance columns in monkey striate cortex an interesting 'example' of the intimate relations between immanent causation, multiplicity, and the rejection of final cause. If one eye of a developing rhesus monkey is closed for a period of time during the first six months of life, the adult will have poor or no depth perception. Of the cells of the visual part of the cerebral cortex, Konner writes, 'These "binoculary responsive cells" prove to be linked up to both eyes through circuitry that develops during the first six months of life . . . , and the strange fact is that these two eyes are in active competition for those linkages—take one out of the competition for even a few days, and the other eye will take over the visual cortex cell completely, ending forever the chance of its responding to both eyes, integrating their slightly different information, and allowing the monkey to see depth.' See Melvin Konner, *The Tangled Wing: Biological Constraints on the Human Spirit* (New York: Holt, Rinehart and Winston, 1982), p. 389.

24. The salvific import of divine immutability in the *Ethic* finds an analogue in Simone Weil's insistence upon the complete absence of mercy as mercy's proof. Of necessity and the good, she writes, 'La nécessité en tant qu'absolument autre que

le bien est le bien lui-même.' In so far as it is absolutely other than the good, necessity is the good itself. See Simone Weil, *La pesanteur et la grâce* (Paris: Librairie Plon, 1948), p. 112. Weil's conception of grace both contradicts and parallels the Spinozistic doctrine. Weil knew Spinoza's work well.

25.   For a good summary of the issues in the nominalist/realist controversy on Spinoza, see Francis S. Haserot, 'Spinoza and the Status of Universals,' in *Studies in Spinoza*, ed. S. Paul Kashap (Berkeley: University of California, 1972), pp. 43–67. Haserot's analysis proves Spinoza a realist.

26.   Ep. 62 from Henry Oldenburg to Spinoza refers to Spinoza's plans to publish the *Ethic*. Ep. 68 from Spinoza to Oldenburg gives Spinoza's reasons for not publishing. See *The Correspondence of Spinoza*, ed. A. Wolf (London: George Allen & Unwin, 1928), pp. 303–04 and pp. 334–35.

27.   cf. *On the Improvement of the Understanding*. 'Whence these fixed and eternal things, though they are themselves particular, will nevertheless, owing to their presence and power everywhere, be to us universals or genera of definitions of particular mutable things, and as the proximate causes of all things.' See *Spinoza Selections*, ed. John Wild (New York: Charles Scribner's Sons, 1958), p. 40, or *Spinoza Opera*, ed. Gebhardt, II, 37, 5. This is a key text.

28.   cf. Ep, 83, which treats the possibility of the derivation of the variety of things *a priori* from extension. See *The Correspondence of Spinoza*, ed. A. Wolf (London: George Allen & Unwin, 1928), p. 365.

29.   In a somewhat different context, Harold Foster Hallett interprets this demonstration in an analogous way. See H. F. Hallett, *Aeternitas* (Oxford: Clarendon Press, 1930), pp. 89–90, note 1.

30.   In *On the Improvement of the Understanding*, Spinoza writes of the necessary truth of simple ideas and their compounds, that is, the ideas deduced from them. Such ideas cannot but be clearly and distinctly conceived. Comparison of these simple ideas with the simples of Descartes' *Rules for the Direction of the Mind* is necessary to the study of Spinoza's works. In the *Ethic*, Spinoza assimilates the simples to his theory of common notions.

The simple natures of Descartes and the common notions of Spinoza are the bases of reason as each conceives it, but the thorough reading of Descartes and Spinoza that reveals the similarity, indeed kinship, of the simples and common notions ends in recognition of their difference and in an understanding of the differing meanings of reason itself in the work of these two rationalists.

31.   cf. *Theologico-Political Treatise*, trans. R. H. M. Elwes (New York: Dover, 1951), p. 270, note 6 or *Spinoza Opera*, ed. Gebhardt, III, 252, 22.

32.   This is H. F. Hallett's interpretation. See H. F. Hallett, *Aeternitas* (Oxford: Clarendon Press, 1930), pp. 100–01.

33.   cf. Harold Henry Joachim, *A Study of the Ethics of Spinoza* (New York: Russell & Russell, 1964), pp. 173–76.

34.   cf. Spinoza's discussion of this theme in *On the Improvement of Understanding* in *Spinoza Selections*, ed. John Wild (New York: Charles Scribner's Sons, 1958), p. 29 ff. and p. 39, or *Spinoza Opera*, ed. Gebhardt, II, 28, 29 and II, 36, 13.

35.   This might describe Thomas Carson Mark's mistake in *Spinoza's Theory of Truth* (New York: Columbia University Press, 1972). See note 22.

36.   Francis S. Haserot in 'Spinoza and the Status of Universals,' correctly summarizes the elements of universality in Spinoza's thought. See *Studies in Spinoza*, ed. S. Paul Kashap (Berkeley: University of California, 1972), p. 66. Haserot does not, however, work through the differences among the various elements. Specifically, he does not contrast concrete and rational universals. Our study tries to clarify these issues.

37.   Spinoza's spectrum of epistemic transcendence may be fruitfully compared with the Platonic line of cognition, a comparison for which we are indebted to Harvey Burstein of Queens College, CUNY. Whatever questions such comparison may raise concerning the autonomous or heteronomous life of mind, we cannot fail to observe the intentional nature of consciousness in both these thinkers.

All consciousness is of an object, and the truest object of consciousness is God/ the Good. At the level of imagination, of flux and impingement, we do not recognize the mind's true object. In so far as we are determined through our own power, we rejoice as knowledge of God. The power of an idea is commensurable with the value of its object. Man becomes more active as the object of his thought becomes more complex, more unified. Here, we see that Spinoza's conception of man as desire, desire realizing itself in knowledge of the most perfect object, is identical to the doctrine of *eros* in Plato's *Symposium*. For Plato, also, we are defined by our object. Our power is commensurable with what we love. Thus, each in his own way, sees the philosopher, the lover of God/the Good, as the highest type of humanity.

For Spinoza, as for Plato, desire is the essence or soul of man. Man's existence is being as becoming. According to the myth of Diotima, Eros is intermediate between mortal and immortal. Unlike the gods, he does not possess the good, but divinity is mixed in him, and he longs for the divine. So Spinoza, in the language of substance and mode, speaks of man's existence as tension between mortal and immortal, between finite and infinite.

38. See *Spinoza's Short Treatise on God, Man, and His Well-Being*, trans. and ed. A. Wolf (London: Adam and Charles Black, 1910), p. 133.

39. Gilles Deleuze writes of a 'hatred of interiority' in Spinoza's philosophy. This one phrase is worth volumes of commentary. See Gilles Deleuze, 'I have nothing to admit,' *Semiotexte*, 2, no. 3 (1977), 112. Deleuze sees Spinoza as opposed to the rationalist tradition, but his reading of Spinoza is acute and valuable.

BIBLIOGRAPHY

Works by Spinoza

Spinoza Opera. Ed. Carl Gebhardt. 4 vols. Heidelberg: C. Winter, 1925.

Translations

Correspondence of Spinoza. Trans. A. Wolf. London: George Allen & Unwin, 1928.
The Ethics and Selected Letters. Trans. Samuel Shirley; ed. Seymore Feldman. Indianapolis: Hackett, 1982.
The Principles of Descartes' Philosophy. Trans. Halbert Hains. Chicago: Open Court, 1905.
Spinoza Selections. Ed. John Wild. New York: Charles Scribner's Sons, 1958. Contains the W. H. White translation of the *Ethic,* the Elwes, Bohn translation of the *Improvement of the Understanding,* and an abridged version of the *Short Treatise,* as well as a selection of letters, in translations by A. Wolf.
Spinoza's Short Treatise on God, Man, and His Well-Being. Trans. and ed. A. Wolf. London: Adam and Charles Black, 1910.
A Theologico-Political Treatise and A Political Treatise. Trans. R. H. M. Elwes. 1883; rpt. New York: Dover, 1951.

Critical Studies and Reference Works

AVENARUIS, RICHARD. *Ueber die beiden ersten Phasen des Spinozischen Pantheismus und das Verhältniss der zweiten zur dritten Phase.* Leipzig: E. Avenarius, 1868.
BACHELARD, GASTON. 'Physique et Metaphysique.' *Septimana Spinozana.* Ed. Societas Spinozanae. The Hague: Martinus Nijhoff, 1933, pp. 74–84.
BENNETT, JONATHAN. *A Study of Spinoza's Ethics.* Indianapolis: Hackett, 1984.
BERNHARDT, JEAN. 'Infini, substance et attributs.' *Cahiers Spinoza,* No. 2 (1978), 53–92.
BOSCHERINI, EMILIA GIANCOTTI. *Lexicon Spinozanum.* 2 vols. Archives internationales d'histoire des idées, 28. The Hague: Martinus Nijhoff, 1970.
BRUNSCHVICG, LEON. 'Le Platonisme de Spinoza.' *Chronicon Spinozanum.* The Hague: Societas Spinozanae. Vol. III, 1923, pp. 253–68.
BURG, EVELYN. 'On Spinoza's Conceptions of Power and Freedom.' Unpbl. ms., 1978.
COLERUS, JOHANNES. *The Life of Benedict de Spinosa. written by John Colerus . . . Done out of French.* London: D. L. and B. Bragg, 1706. [An English translation of *La vie de Spinosa par Jean Colerus.* The Hague: T. Johnson, 1706.]
COOLEY, WILLIAM F. 'Spinoza's Pantheistic Argument.' *Studies in The History of Ideas.* New York: Columbia University Press, 1918, pp. 171–87.
CURLEY, EDWIN M. *Spinoza's Metaphysics: An Essay in Interpretation.* Cambridge, Mass.: Harvard U. Press, 1969.
DE DIJN, HERMAN. 'Historical Remarks on Spinoza's Theory of Definition.' *Spinoza on Knowing, Being and Freedom.* Ed. J. G. Van der Bend. Assen: Van Gorcum & Co., 1974, pp. 41–50.
DELBOS, VICTOR. 'La notion de substance et la notion de dieu dans la philosphie de Spinoza.' *Revue de métaphysique et de morale,* No. 6 (1908) 783–88.
DELEUZE, GILLES. *Spinoza.* Paris: Presses universitaires de France, 1970.
——. *Spinoza et la problème de l'expression.* Paris: Les Éditions de Minuit, 1968.
DEREGIBUS, ARTURO. *La Dottrina de Spinoza sull'infinito.* Vol. II of *Bruno e Spinoza, La realtà dell'infinito e il problema della sua unità.* Turin: Giapichelli, 1981.
DEWEY, JOHN. 'The Pantheism of Spinoza.' *Journal of Speculative Philosophy,* 16 (1882), 249–57.

ERDMANN, JOHANN EDUARD. *Grundriss der Geschichte der Philosophie*. Berlin: Wilhelm Hertz, Vol. II, 1870, pp. 45–74.

FORSYTH, T. M. 'Spinoza's Doctrine of God in Relation to His Conception of Causality.' *Studies in Spinoza: Critical and Interpretive Essays*. Ed. S. Paul Kashap. Berkeley: U. of California Press, 1972, pp. 3–15.

FREUDENTHAL, JACOB, ed. *Die Lebensgeschichte Spinoza's in Quellenschriften, Urkunden und nichtamlichen Nachrichten*. Preussischen Akademie der Wissenschaften. Leipzig: Veit, 1899.

——. *Spinoza, Leben und Lehre*. Vol. V of *Bibliotheca Spinozana*. Ed. Carl Gebhardt. Heidelberg: C. Winter, 1927.

GEBHARDT, CARL. *Inedita Spinoza*. Heidelberg: C. Winter, 1916.

——. 'Spinoza und der Platonismus.' *Chronicon Spinozanum*. The Hague: Societas Spinozanae. Vol. I, 1921, 178–234.

GUERET, MICHEL, et al., eds. *Spinoza, Ethica; concordances, index, listes de fréquences, tables comparatives*. Louvain-la-Neuve, Belgium: Publications du CETEDOC, Université Catholique de Louvain, 1977.

GUEROULT, MARTIAL. *Spinoza*. 2 vols. Paris: Editions Montaigne and Editions Aubier-Montaigne, 1968, 1974; Hildesheim, George Olms, co-ed., 1968, 1974.

——. 'Spinoza's Letter on the Infinite.' *Spinoza: A Collection of Critical Essays*. Ed. Marjorie Grene. Garden City, New York: Doubleday, 1973, pp. 182–212.

HALLETT, HAROLD FOSTER. *Aeternitas: A Spinozistic Study*. Oxford: Clarendon Press, 1930.

——. *Benedict de Spinoza: The Elements of His Philosophy*. London: Athlone Press, 1957.

——. *Creation, Emanation and Salvation: A Spinozistic Study*. The Hague: Martinus Nijhoff, 1962.

——. 'On a Reputed Equivoque in the Philosophy of Spinoza.' In Kashap, ed., *Studies in Spinoza*, pp. 168–88.

——. 'Spinoza's Conception of Eternity.' *Mind*, NS 37 (1928), 283–303.

——. 'Substance and Its Modes.' In Grene, ed., *Spinoza: Critical Essays*, pp. 131–63.

HAMPSHIRE, STUART. *Spinoza*. New York, Penguin, 1951.

——. *Two Theories of Morality*. Oxford: Oxford U. Press, 1977.

HARDIN, C. L. 'Spinoza on Immortality and Time.' *Spinoza: New Perspectives*. Ed. Robert W. Shahan and J. I. Biro. Norman, Okla.: U. of Oklahoma Press, 1978, pp. 129–38.

HARRIS, ERROL E. 'The Order and Connection of Ideas.' In Van der Bend, ed., *Spinoza on Knowing, Being and Freedom*, pp. 103–13.

——. *Salvation from Despair: A Reappraisal of Spinoza's Philosophy*. The Hague: Martinus Nijhoff, 1973.

——. 'Spinoza's Theory of Human Immortality.' *The Monist*, 55, No. 4 (1971), 668–85.

HART, ALAN. *Spinoza's Ethics Part I & II, A Platonic Commentary*. Leiden: E. J. Brill, 1983.

HASEROT, FRANCIS S. 'Spinoza and the Status of Universals.' In Kashap, ed., *Studies in Spinoza*, pp. 43–67.

——. 'Spinoza's Definition of Attribute.' In Kashap, ed., *Studies in Spinoza*, pp. 28–42.

HUBBELING, H. G. 'The Discussions at the Spinoza-Symposium in Amersfoort, September 10–13, 1973.' In Van der Bend, ed., *Spinoza on Knowing, Being and Freedom*, pp. 184–88.

HUNT, JOHN. *An Essay on Pantheism*, rev. ed. London: Gibbings, 1893, pp. 219–42.

HYMAN, ARTHUR. 'Spinoza's Dogmas of Universal Faith in the Light of their Medieval Jewish Background.' *Biblical and Other Studies*. Ed. A. Altman. Cambridge, Mass.: Harvard University Press, 1963, pp. 183–95.

JOACHIM, HAROLD HENRY. *Spinoza's Tractatus de intellectus emendatione*. Oxford: Clarendon Press, 1958.

——. *A Study of the Ethics of Spinoza*. New York: Russell & Russell, 1964.

JONAS, HANS. 'Spinoza and the theory of Organism.' In Grene, ed., *Spinoza: Critical Essays*, pp. 259–78.

JONES, WILLIAM THOMAS. *A History of Western Philosophy*. New York: Harcourt, Brace and World, Vol. III, 1952, pp. 192–218.

KASHAP, S. PAUL. 'Spinoza's Use of "Idea".' In Kashap, ed., *Spinoza: New Perspectives*, pp. 57–70.

KETTNER, FREDERICK. 'The Hentheism of Spinoza.' *The Spinoza Quarterly*, 2, No. 2 (1932), pp. 34–43.
——. *Spinoza The Biosopher.* New York: Roerich Museum Press, 1932.
KRISTELLER, PAUL OSKAR. 'Stoic and Neoplatonic Sources of Spinoza's *Ethics.' History of European Ideas*, 5, No. 1 (1984), 1–15.
LACHTERMAN, DAVID R. 'The Physics of Spinoza's *Ethics.'* In Shahan and Biro, eds., *Spinoza: New Perspectives*, pp. 71–112.
MACINTYRE, ALISDAIR. 'Pantheism.' *Encyclopedia of Philosophy.* New York: Macmillan, 1967.
——. 'Spinoza.' *Encyclopedia of Philosophy.* New York: Macmillan, 1967.
MARK, THOMAS CARSON. *Spinoza's Theory of Truth.* New York: Columbia U. Press, 1972.
——. 'Truth and Adequacy in Spinozistic Ideas.' In Shahan and Biro, eds., *Spinoza: New Perspectives*, pp. 11–34.
MARTINEAU, JAMES. *A Study of Spinoza.* London: Macmillan, 1882.
MCKEON, RICHARD. *The Philosophy of Spinoza: The Unity of His Thought.* New York: Longmans, Green & Co., 1928.
MILNER, SIMON L. *The Face of Benedictus Spinoza.* New York: Machmadim Art Editions, 1946.
MOLTKE, S. GRAM. 'Spinoza, Substance, and Predication.' *Theoria*, 34 (1968), 222–44.
NAESS, ARNE. 'Is Freedom Consistent with Spinoza's Determinism?' In Van der Bend, ed., *Spinoza on Knowing, Being and Freedom*, pp. 6–23.
OKO, ADOLPH. *The Spinoza Bibliography.* Boston: G. K. Hall, 1964.
PARKINSON, G. H. R. 'Spinoza on the Power and Freedom of Man.' *The Monist*, 55, No. 4 (1971), 527–53.
——. *Spinoza's Theory of Knowledge.* Oxford: Clarendon Press, 1954.
PICTON, JAMES ALLANSON. *Pantheism: its story and significance.* London: Constable, 1914.
PLUMPTRE, CONSTANCE. *General Sketch of the History of Pantheism.* 2 vols. London, Gibbings, 1878.
POLLOCK, FREDERICK. *Spinoza: His Life and Philosophy.* 2nd ed. New York: American Scholar Publications, 1966.
POWELL, ELMER ELLSWORTH. *Spinoza and Religion.* Chicago: Open Court, 1906.
PRÉPOSIET, JEAN. *Bibliographie Spinoziste.* Annales Littéraires de l'Université de Besançon, 154. Paris: Les Belles Lettres, 1973.
RITCHIE, ELIZA. 'Notes on Spinoza's Conception of God.' *The Philosophical Review*, 11, No. 1 (1902), 1–15.
——. 'The Reality of the Finite in Spinoza's System.' *The Philosophical Review*, 13, No. 1 (1904), 16–29.
RIVAUD, ALBERT. *Les notions d'essence et d'existence dans la philosophie de Spinoza.* Paris: Alcan, 1905.
——. 'Quelques remarques sur la notion d'essence dans les doctrines de Descartes et de Spinoza.' *Septimana Spinozana.* Ed. Societas Spinozanae. The Hague: Martinus Nijhoff, 1933, pp. 208–25.
ROBINSON, LEWIS. *Kommentar zu Spinozas Ethik.* Leipzig: Felix Meiner, 1928.
SERVAAS VAN ROOIJEN, ABRAHAM JACOBUS. *Inventaire des livres formant la bibliothèque de Benedict Spinoza.* The Hague: W. C. Tengeler, 1888.
SIWEK, PAUL. *Spinoza et le panthéisme religieux.* Paris: Brouwer, 1937.
STRAUSS, LEO. *Persecution and the Art of Writing.* Glencoe, Ill.: The Free Press, 1952.
THOMAS, KARL. *Spinoza's Individualismus und Pantheismus.* Konigsberg: A. Samter, 1848.
VOLKELT, JOHANNES. *Pantheismus und Individualismus im Systeme Spinoza's.* Leipzig: A. Lorentz, 1872.
VULLIAUD, PAUL. *Spinoza d'après les livres de sa bibliothèque.* Paris: Bibliothèque Chacornac, 1934.
WEINBURG, KURT. 'Pantheismusstreit.' *Encyclopedia of Philosophy.* New York: Macmillan, 1967.
WETLESEN, JON. *A Spinoza Bibliography 1940–1967.* Oslo: Universitetforlaget, 1968.
WIENPAHL, PAUL. *The Radical Spinoza.* New York: NYU Press, 1979.
WINDELBAND, WILHELM. *A History of Philosophy.* Trans. James H. Tufts. 2nd ed. New York: Macmillan, 1901.
WOLF, A., trans and ed. *The Oldest Biography of Spinoza.* Attributed to Jean Maximilien

Lucas. London: George Allen & Unwin, 1927. [Originally published in Hamburg in 1735 as *La vie de Spinosa*.]

——. 'Spinoza's Conception of the Attributes of Substance.' In Kashap, ed., *Studies in Spinoza*, pp. 16–27.

WOLFSON, HARRY AUSTRYN. *The Philosophy of Spinoza*. 2 vols. 1934; rpt. New York: Schocken, 1969.

INDEX